9-68

MINNESOTA BIBLE COLLEGE
LIBRARY.

DATE DUE

Crossroads College
G.H. Cachiaras Memorial Library
920 Mayowood Road SW, Rochester MN 5
507-535-3331

EMERGENT VOICE

EMERGENT VOICE

By

Kenneth N. Westerman

Mus.B., A.B., M.A., Sc.D.

782.04
~~762~~
~~E77~~
W 5273
13606

Mailing Address
CAROL F. WESTERMAN
Box 62
Ann Arbor, Michigan

Copyright 1947
KENNETH N. WESTERMAN
Second Edition
Copyright 1955
The Heirs of Kenneth N. Westerman

Lithographed in U.S.A. by
E D W A R D S   B R O T H E R S ,   I N C .
Ann Arbor, Michigan

Sept. 20, 1968

H. O.

music

DEDICATED
to my wife and our
two daughters
JEAN and MIRIAM
whose
sacrifice, enthusiasm, and loyalty
have made possible
the scientific investigations
which have verified its simple truths;

and

to that vast throng of students
who have wished to know the "why" and "how" of their
emerging voices.

KENNETH N. WESTERMAN

Foreword

ONE of our clearest modern thinkers says, "We must remember that knowledge has widened and deepened, so that, could any of us really catch up with the information of our own time, he would have little temptation to indulge the mediaeval habit of appealing to the authority of the past." [1]

The voice teaching profession is at the beginning of its final development, the era of examined data. It has passed the infancy of *imitation,* the youth of *empirical findings,* and is now starting on the maturity of *scientific investigation* through the use of the phonograph, amplifier, cathode ray oscillograph, high speed camera, X-ray, harmonic analyser, galvanometer, kymograph, stroboscope, auto-laryngoscope, and all the other aids to the voice scientist which electrical and engineering research have developed.

EMERGENT VOICE represents the accumulation of the present knowledge of voice teaching by careful correlation of the known facts in the fields of anatomy, physiology, neurology, psychology, embryology, endocrinology, physics, sound engineering, acoustics, phonetics, biolinguistics, speech, speech reading, and singing.

This vast amount of research, followed by a thorough review of existing voice literature, has given the author a clear insight into the fundamentals of voice teaching. The techniques presented in EMERGENT VOICE are simple, easily understood, and quickly applied by both teacher and student. To that throng whose joy of living is increased through self-expression in singing, EMERGENT VOICE makes a lasting contribution.

[1] Robinson, James Harvey. *The Mind in the Making.* New York: Harper and Bros.

TABLE OF CONTENTS

Dedication v

Foreword vii

Introduction xi

CHAPTER

   I. The Study of Voice 3

  II. Singing and Speaking 11

 III. Posture and Respiration 15

  IV. Phonation 29

   V. Resonation 37

  VI. Articulation 47

 VII. Humming 73

VIII. Exercises 81

  IX. Developing the Speaking Voice 105

   X. Theory: Basic Rhythms 109

  XI. Theory: Melodic and Harmonic Reading 125

 XII. Lä-mī-nō-zation 139

XIII. The Boy's Voice 143

XIV. Interpretation and Literature 147

      Bibliography of American Folk Songs 154

      Addendum Vibrato 161

      Bibliography 169

Introduction

EMERGENT VOICE is what the name implies—a study of how the human voice emerges from the body. It is not just a new name for voice production, but is written because the author has a profound belief that voice teachers must take into full consideration the causative muscle movements in voice training if they are to be of real service to their students.

When a child is born, the whole framework for singing is written in his life processes of breathing, sucking, and swallowing. The normal functioning of his nutrition, moving muscles, secreting glands, and nerve reactions make singing as natural to him as barking to dogs, lowing to cattle, or singing to birds.

EMERGENT VOICE has for its aim the presentation of the physiological emergence of the human voice in the three fields of Skills, Theory, and Literature. The author hopes that its written language will be so direct and natural that the vast throng of adolescent youth, young manhood and womanhood, and adults, who wish to express their thoughts, emotions, passions, and moods, can find a normal, healthy outlet in the free and natural use of their own voices in singing.

It has long been an accepted fact that "He who behaves as tissue behaves, becomes free" [1] and the author of EMERGENT VOICE knows that students can find perfect freedom in singing through patterning and conditioning of the normal actions of posture, respiration, phonation, resonation, and articulation into a blended whole.

The author has tried to express the principles of voice emergence in a language that will give the student a vision of the balanced flexibility of the bodily functions which combine in producing the most flexible and beautiful of musical instruments—the human voice.

Acknowledgment is made to Professor Clarence L. Meader, the founder of the Biolinguistic Department of the University of Michigan for his vision that "All structures arise from previously existing structures and all processes as modifications of previously existing functions." Profound gratitude is expressed to Doctor John Henry Muyskens, Professor of Phonetics and Director of the Biolinguistic Laboratories at the University of Michigan, for his constant inspiration as chairman of the author's doctoral committee in the Horace H. Rackham School of Graduate Studies while the author was correlating the findings of the

---

[1] Muyskens, John Henry. Class Lecture. Biolinguistic Department, University of Michigan, 1937.

thirteen fields bearing on the teaching of vocal techniques. The patience and enthusiasm of Doctor Leon Henri Strong of the University of Michigan Medical School were of inestimable worth in helping to build, in the author, a scientific foundation from which he could examine and combine the knowledge of the singing processes already known to the fields of anatomy, neurology, physiology, speech, phonetics, and bio-linguistics, with those of the voice teaching profession.

Much of the work in the chapter on Theory and Literature is the personal contribution of my wife. Without her inspiration and sacrifice the scientific investigations, which made EMERGENT VOICE possible, could not have been made.

KENNETH N. WESTERMAN
Ann Arbor, Michigan, 1946

Introduction to the Second Edition

KENNETH N. WESTERMAN passed away suddenly on April 22, 1955, just after completing the revisions for this second edition.

He felt, that in these eight years since the first publication, he had seen the spread of these scientific findings more than he had thought possible during his lifetime.

Because of the simplicity of the Exercises in EMERGENT VOICE, some people are inclined to continue using exercises they have learned elsewhere. I would urge the reader to try those in this book, taking every care to apply them accurately. They are carefully planned and one of the most important things in the book.

It is my hope that all, who knew and loved my husband, will inspire others to know the framework of developmental growth and the physiological framework of singing; and that this knowledge will enable many singers to enjoy a greater freedom of expression in song.

CAROL F. WESTERMAN
Ann Arbor, Michigan, July, 1955.

INSTRUCTIONS WITH PLATE I

Breath is drawn low in the lungs (L) by the descending action of the diaphragm (D-D') which causes the protrusion of the abdomen (A-A'). The supporting action of the abdominal muscles shown in Fig. II causes the expiration action of A' to A in Fig. I, but the resistance of the diaphragm (D-D') controls the breath as it passes from the lungs (L) through the large bronchial tubes (LBT). From there it passes through the trachea (T) into the larynx (Lx) where the resistance of the closed vocal cords (VC) [See Plate III-A] converts the breath into tones. These tonal vibrations are transmitted through all tissues to the bony structure of the head and chest. They also travel upward past the epiglottis (Ep) through the pharynx (Px) into the naso-pharynx (NPx) and nasal cavities (NC). Here the overtones are partially absorbed and the fundamental strengthened, adding a dark, rich, ringing quality to the voice. The mouth (M) by means of the action of the jaw (J), tongue (Tng), and lips (Ls) converts the tones into vowels and consonants, and the reinforcement of these tones transmitting through the tissues into the hard palate (HP) and the bony structures of the head, *adds power and brilliance to the voice.* The uvula (U-U'), root of the tongue (Tng), and larynx (Lx) rise on high pitches and lower on low pitches; and by the transmission of vibrations through the tissues of the resonator (solid black), all of the bony structures surrounding the brain cavity (BC), including the turbinate bones (TB) and the sinuses (S), cause the resounding of tone vibrations, known as the resonance of the human voice.

PLATE No. I

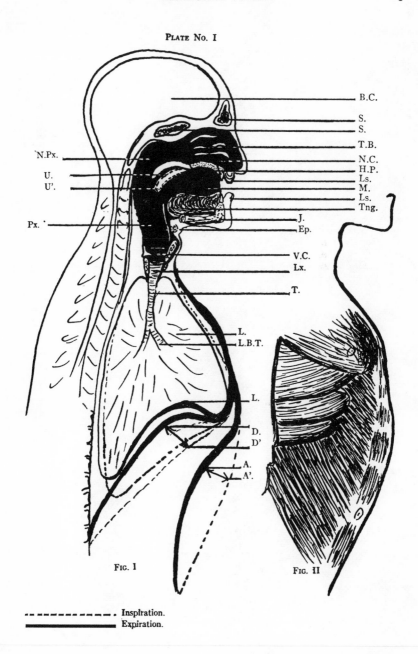

B.C.
S.
S.
T.B.
N.C.
H.P.
Ls.
M.
Ls.
Tng.
J.
Ep.
V.C.
Lx.
T.
L.
L.B.T.
L.
D.
D'
A.
A'.

N.Px.
U.
U'.
Px.

Fig. I   Fig. II

– – – – – – – – – Inspiration.
————————— Expiration.

CHAPTER I

THE STUDY OF VOICE

E VERY student who expects to fully enjoy the use of his voice must develop not only foundational (1) SKILLS in singing, but a practical working knowledge of musical (2) THEORY, and a basic understanding of the art of singing through a study of its folk (3) LITERATURE.

EMERGENT VOICE is not written on a lesson plan basis but with the three main divisions of Skills [Chapters I to IX], Theory [Chapters X to XIII], and Literature [Chapter XIV], in a separate progressive development. The ability to sing, to read music at sight, and to interpret musical literature may thus be co-ordinated and developed as fast as the ability of the individual or group makes it possible. EMERGENT VOICE will be effective only as the teacher and student follow the techniques used in the development of Skills, Theory, and Literature in their progressive order and with a basic knowledge of the "why" and "how" of each new technique.

SKILLS

In the past, the study of *skills* in singing has been primarily a study of *tone*. EMERGENT VOICE *is written on the working hypothesis that the study of skills in singing is not primarily the study of tone, but the study of the effect upon tone of the muscle movements used in posture, respiration, phonation, resonation, and articulation as the tone emerges from the human body.*

The student who wishes to make intelligent and rapid development in the beauty and flexibility of his voice needs a knowledge of how that voice emerges. He must have a framework upon which to build the techniques which blend his natural body actions into voice emergence.

Singing is the result of the combined blending of five body actions into a balanced flexibility which we call the human voice. Although these actions, by their blending and overlapping, become the single unit which we recognize as voice, each action is responsible for the freedom and efficiency of the next. In the order of emergence they are: Posture, Respiration, Phonation, Resonation, and Articulation.

Without good (1) posture, (2) respiration (breathing) cannot be efficient for singing purposes. Without controlled respiration, (3) phonation (tone production) cannot be clear. Without clear phonation, (4) resonation (the resounding of tone vibrations within the cavities and from the bony structures of the head) cannot be full, and free from muscle interference; and without full and free resonation, (5) articulation (the pronouncing of words) cannot be accurate and distinct. There is no escape from this framework. *Posture is its foundation and articulation is the end product.*

Physiologically the human voice literally *emerges* from our bodies. The muscular actions of (1) posture assist those of (2) respiration. The muscle movements of (2) respiration are the source of (3) phonation. Clear (3) phonation is a distinct help in fuller (4) resonation, while adequate (4) resonation permits ease and freedom of (5) articulation. These five muscular activities, by their overlapping and blending, become the single unit which we call the human voice.

Beautiful voices are built, and natural voices increased in range, power, and flexibility by the use of techniques and exercises designed to assist in the blending and freedom of the muscle actions involved in this emergence. Any attempt on the part of the teacher or student to reverse the order, results in muscle blockings and interferences and the voice loses its beauty. Corrections of interference and blocking must be done from the gross muscles of posture toward the smaller muscles of articulation.

VIBRATO (See Illustration No. I)

If the student is to grasp the full significance of the framework of EMERGENT VOICE, he must now have definite knowledge of the part vibrato plays in voice development.

When a person sings freely, with a balanced, flexible use of all the muscles of posture, respiration, phonation, resonation, and articulation, the human voice has in it a slight, regular pulsation called vibrato. The author's investigations in the causes of vibrato[1] have shown that this pulsation is a blending of three types: (1) a pulsation of loudness and softness, which arises from the balanced, flexible use of respiratory controls, called intensity or amplitude vibrato; (2) a pulsation of two pitches, which arises from the muscular controls of clear tone production, called pitch or rate vibrato; and (3) a pulsation of changing relationship of fundamental and overtones, arising from the physical structure of the two pulsing pitches, called timbre or complexity vibrato.

Vibrato is like one's heart beat—*it is something which cannot be taught.* It is slow and light when you are lax, and fast and strong when you are tense. It varies with the activities of the muscles of your body. Contrary to past beliefs, it has nothing to do with emotional strain except as emotional strain uses muscle tensions, which in turn,

---

[1] Westerman, Kenneth N. *Vibrato, A Specific Integrational Emergence Upon Fusure of Somatic Rhythms.* Doctoral thesis, University of Michigan, 1939. See Addendum for the epitome of this thesis.

of necessity have to use faster and stronger nerve pulses. Vibrato is the reflection in the human voice of the basic nerve pulse rate which runs the muscles of posture and from which the activity of muscle action emerges. With heart beat and breath pulse it constitutes the triumvirate of body rhythms which runs the framework of posture, respiration, phonation, resonation, and articulation.

Vibrato runs the muscles of the whole animal kingdom. Tonus, physiological tremor, shaking palsy, the shaking edge of a newspaper held tensely in one position, hysterical tremor from shell shock, a goat bleat, the quavering call of a screech owl, the shivering of a dog on a cold day, are all, like vibrato in the human voice, manifestations of this same nerve pulse, under normal or abnormal conditions. Without vibrato (physiologists call it *tonus*) one could not stand erect. If under sickness or disease, vibrato (tonus) leaves the muscles, one is unable to raise his head from the pillow, he ceases to be able to stand erect, finally even his eyes cease to focus, and he passes into coma and death. When it

A

B

C

ILLUSTRATION I

VIBRATO

A. E vowel vibrato at slow speed.
B. Same vibrato at high speed and great amplitude showing the form at an antinode.
C. Same vibrato at high speed showing form at the node.

starts to break down in old age, it becomes shaking palsy. During sleep it loses its regular activity.

The vibrato rate in the human voice is the basic rate of the nerve pulses (action currents) that keep the body in tonic condition. These pulses become faster during exercise. Whenever any two sets of muscles used in singing are perfectly balanced in their work, vibrato rates remain normal. Whenever muscles strain against each other, vibrato becomes clinical or exaggerated. The voice teaching profession calls such vibratos *tremolos*. The writer dislikes the term. It is still vibrato. We should learn to designate vibrato as *good* or *bad, normal* or *clinical, fast* or *slow, wide* or *narrow, fine* or *exaggerated*. If the student has a normal vibrato, it doesn't need to be mentioned. If the student has a clinical vibrato, it doesn't need to be mentioned. *Don't teach vibrato.* Teach easy, balanced, flexible muscle actions and vibrato will take care of itself. Vibrato in the human voice is both a cause and a result. When, by normal overlapping, blending, and balanced, flexible use, muscle action is at its best for efficient control, vibrato is normal, for it efficiently runs the muscle actions and efficiently shows its work in the resulting tone.

Every artist has vibrato in his singing voice, not because he developed vibrato, but because the nerve pulses which run his muscles are at vibrato rates when he uses those muscles efficiently. He cannot keep it out of his voice. He can sing "Old Black Joe" lazily, and these pulses, like heart beat, will slow up, or he can use such a powerful energy surge from his abdominal wall on the climax of the "Toreador Song" that they will speed up, but he cannot stop his vibrato as long as he sings a clear tone, fully resonated. It is as much a part of his voice as his breathing or his heart beat.

Even when we do violent exercise and these nerve pulses speed up to 20, 40, 50, or 100 per second, still in the background of our muscles are the vibrato pulses (action currents) of 5, 6, or 7 per second, maintaining posture and poise for the work. The human body is controlled by pairs of contrasting muscles which work against each other: the diaphragm against the abdominal lift; the minute vocal muscle fibers against the weight of the thyro-arytenoids; the muscles from the soft palate to the sides of the tongue and throat against those from the palate to the base of the skull; the longitudinal muscles of the tongue against the circular muscles of the tongue. There are about forty-five chances for clinical vibratos to develop in the emergent framework of posture, respiration, phonation, resonation, articulation, and facial expressions, as against one chance of perfect overlapping and blending of all the muscles involved. Starting with high chest breathing (which forces tensions throughout the vocal track), running the full gamut of interferences clear through to the fighting of two closely related vowel forms in the actions of the tongue, one finds many possibilities for clinical vibrato. In fact, the use of gross skeletal muscles for purposes other than posture, any place in the framework of voice emergence, seems to cause tensions which result in exaggerated vibratos.

A normal vibrato is a decided asset to the vocalist. It is the "thrill of the voice." Violinists imitate it to keep their tone from being colorless. It is the fastest rate for scale singing. It is the normal pulse of a trill. With the heart beat and breath pulse it forms the triumvirate of body rhythms; all our rhythmic patterns are developed from combinations of the three.

A student should not try to build a vibrato into his voice. He should sing with such poise; such easy, flexible muscle actions; such a nicety of balance in muscular controls, that a normal vibrato emerges. Then don't pay any attention to it. Interpret your song. Your vibrato will take care of itself. It is your nerve pulse energy for easy singing. You cannot stand with a good posture and sing clearly and beautifully without it, for it runs your voice.

TECHNIQUES

There are only three types of techniques which can be used by the teacher or student in the development of the emergent framework of posture, respiration, phonation, resonation, and articulation. There are techniques of (1) **Physiology,** which have to do with the muscle movements involved in the blended acts of singing; techniques of (2) **Physics,** which have their foundation in the laws of sound; and techniques of (3) **Psychology,** based on mental reactions in emotions, passions, moods, and the thoughts of the teacher and student as they listen to the emerging voice.

To the student, *as a producer,* all of these techniques are physiological, for he cannot hear his own voice until after it is produced and any changes in its emergence must be brought about by changes of muscle movements.

It is difficult to state, in simple terms, the framework of a philosophy of teaching which must use facts from the three sciences of physiology, physics, and psychology for its techniques. The tones produced by the vocal folds are the result of physiological actions. Once produced, they obey the laws of sound. When used to express thoughts, emotions, passions, and moods they become the instrument of mind.

The aim of every student of voice should be to build a voice of such flexibility and beauty that it will respond instantly to the slightest change of thought or emotion, as the student interprets the text of each song.

The process by which co-ordinated physiological actions develop to interpretation level, so that the vocal student can sing involuntarily, has been revealed by the research of Dr. Viola A. Brody.[2] This develop-

---

[2] Brody, Viola A. *An Experimental Study of the Emergence of the Process Involved in the Production of Song.* Doctoral Dissertation, Univ. of Mich., 1947.

mental growth emerges through four levels. Whatever the age of the individual, *any* new physiological action starts somewhere in that framework and goes through the developmental process from there on.

I. VIABILITY LEVEL. *Energy,* furnished through nutrition and mobilized by the blood, glands, and viscera from conception to adult life, is designated as the age of *Viability.* It takes energy to grow, move, sing, or speak. Whatever the age, developmental growth starts at the level of *Viability* for without the distributed energy developed through the processes of nutrition, the human body could not function.

II. CO-ORDINATION LEVEL. The use of that energy for growth and muscle movement brings us to the *Co-ordination* level. This is the moving stage. However faulty the co-ordination may be, muscular activity is impossible without energy from the *Viability* level.

III. EPICRITICAL LEVEL. The movement of our bodies makes us aware of the sensations produced. This is known as the *Epicritical* level. This is the feeling stage. Without energy from the *Viability* level and the movement of the *Co-ordination* level we could have no sensations of which to be aware.

IV. ASSOCIATIVE LEVEL. When these sensations, resulting from movement, are reported to the highest centers of the brain in the normal individual, we arrive at *Associative* level. With the awareness and interpretation of body movement, the cycle from muscle to brain and back to muscle is complete, and when any act of the human body is reported from muscle to brain and back to muscle enough times, then the human brain becomes a mind as far as that act is concerned and one can invoke that movement at will. This is the interpretation stage.

In practically all physiological actions, except singing, we have an instant recognition of the simple fact that we cannot work at associative level without coming up through the preceding development. We may, as an adult, start the study of voice at co-ordination level or at epicritical, but only in the most rare instances of the so-called perfect natural voice would we be starting the student's training at associative level. Even then many details of singing would of necessity have to be started with a study of the co-ordination of the muscle actions involved. To expect the mind to run the voice of a student whose co-ordination is still faulty is like expecting a tennis player's mind to make him serve aces before the form of serving has developed from co-ordination, through epicritical, to associative level.

Thus we see that singing is not a special gift of the few, but, like speech, is an emergent growth possible to all. The vision of every voice teacher should be that the normal equipment of birth has in it the possibilities of emergence into beautiful singing, and he should strive to equip himself so he can bring that emergence to its full fruition.

For the student to arrive at this final and completely artistic level of interpretation demands a teacher with a thorough knowledge of technical training in the co-ordinated muscle actions of posture, respiration, phonation, resonation, and articulation and with the infinite patience to inspire the student to develop these co-ordinated acts of singing up through the four levels of energy (viability), muscle movements (co-ordination), carefully analyzed sensations (epicritical) through to freedom in interpretation (associative level).

The student, who, by eager, persistent, careful work, develops complete freedom and vital ease in singing; a thoroughly competent musicianship; a love of poetry; a joy in presenting his own thoughts, emotions, passions, and moods; a repertoire adequate for meeting the opportunities which come as his musical experience unfolds; need not worry about the end of his musical career. He will have such joyful and exhilarating experiences, on the road, that he will finally discover the most basic law of artistic development:—*The journey is more fun than arriving at the goal.*

CHAPTER II

SINGING AND SPEAKING

THE more the facts of developmental growth are revealed, the more we realize the close correlation between singing and speaking. One of the most significant observations the author has made is that *we sing before we speak.* One of the earliest sounds an infant makes, after his initial cry at birth, is the contented soft humming sound he uses as he nurses or when he lies full and happy in his cradle. The sign for that hum is the letter "m." (See Chapter VII, Humming.) In the infant's use of that hum, it has been found in pitch from "A" below middle "C" to the "G" above middle "C." The data to date shows that as he becomes full he flats a semitone. In an adult this same hum becomes our colloquial yes—"m-hm" and the long drawn out "m-m" when we have a mouthful of delicious food.

Another early step in the infant's voice growth is singing the "ä" vowel. This singing practice has been observed ranging from "A" below middle "C" to the high "F♯." In families where singing is a constant experience from birth, this singing ability is never lost and many children even sing melodies *with words* before they talk. When the hum and the "ä" come together the word "Mamma" is formed and everybody is happy, but the baby doesn't know he has said anything. That the whole animal kingdom are *mammals,* and the old Latin word for breasts was also "mamma," would seem to be derivations from the same source.

Both singing and speaking are modifications of the simple, life-giving actions of breathing, valving, sucking, chewing, and swallowing.

When one compares singing with speaking, he is first impressed with their similarities. These are so marked that modern voice teaching bases many of its techniques on the co-ordination of the singing and speaking voice. Techniques for *artistic* singing, however, are based on modifications of speech as well as on similarities.

Speech seldom rests on a single pitch, but is constantly flexing up and down with its rising and falling inflections, accents, and cadences, while singing uses *sustained* pitches. Most *speaking* climaxes are developed within the phrase or the sentence, but *singing* crescendos and decrescendos often lie within the scope of a single tone. Phrases in speaking are mostly of 3 to 10 seconds duration. The same phrases, when sung, may last from 10 to 30 seconds. These modifications demand a more accurate and exact *breath control* for singing than for speaking. Thus a study of *respiration* and a knowledge of techniques of *posture* and *breath control* become the first basic change in voice emergence to artistic singing.

Although a breathy voice is capable of lasting through the ordinary length of a spoken phrase, it cannot last through the longer phrases used in singing. In this we find the reason for the singer developing techniques for *clear tone* as the second change from speech. Simple and exact techniques in the actions of phonation are necessary for the development of clear tone.

Speech, particularly with the English speaking race, is a means of rapid communication, and beauty is not generally recognized as its main asset, although it should be; but singing without beauty would be like poetry without rhythm—its basic element would be lacking. Beauty of tone, whether in instruments or in voice, depends upon the resounding of the tone vibrations within some cavity or cavities, or in vibration of some structure set in motion by the tone, increasing its power and beauty. This resounding of tone vibrations is called *resonance.* The muscular activity which assists in the shaping of the throat so that the tone vibrations can acquire their fullest resonance, is called *resonation.* Resonation is the third modification of speech to make singing reach its higher plane of pure artistry.

The greatest modification from ordinary speech comes in the singing of words. In speech, the overlapping and blending of consonants and vowels are never at rest. Larynx, vocal folds, throat, soft palate, jaw, tongue, cheeks, and lips are constantly shifting as each action affects the action of that preceding and following. In artistic singing the vowel form is pure, the consonants clean and clear; and so in *articulation* we find our fourth modification of speech.

Techniques for the development of these four modifications constitute the means for the emergence of the human voice from speech to artistic singing, for in many families singing is lost when speech begins and singing must be relearned. As both singing and speaking emerged through modifications of breathing, valving, sucking, chewing, and swallowing into the balanced, flexible use of respiration, phonation, resonation, and articulation in the infant, so artistic singing has emerged through the further modification of the overlapping and blending of those same physiological actions.

Until those modifications become so automatic that they may be used without conscious control, the singer's voice will still interfere with his attempts at artistic production instead of being a glorious instrument of interpretation. The study of voice should be an enthusiastic striving for the attainment of such perfect freedom in singing, that the slightest change in the thoughts, emotions, passions, or moods of the singer will find instant reflection in his voice. This is only possible when the overlapping and blending of the balanced, flexible use of the physiological actions of posture, respiration, phonation, resonation, and articulation have emerged into the single unit of a free and fully resonated voice.

It is the hope of the author that developing young artists, through freedom in self-expression, can make their contributions to the happiness of those who hear them, through contagious emotional enthusiasm in the interpretation of their songs.

PLATE II

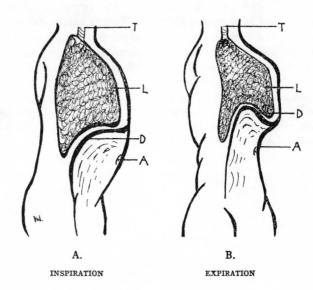

A.   B.

INSPIRATION   EXPIRATION

Figures A and B.   T—trachea   D—diaphragm
                L—lungs   A—abdominal wall

INSTRUCTIONS FOR PLATE II

It is essential that there be no mistake in the student's mind concerning the two views of Plate II. Illustration A is marked INSPIRATION. It shows the body expanded around the waist line as it is when the bottom of the lungs have filled through *diaphragm descent*. Illustration B is marked EXPIRATION. It shows the body at the end of expiration, after the abdominal lift, vocal lips, and diaphragm resistance have used up all available breath for singing or speech.

Do not confuse high chest *inspiration*, resulting from throwing back the shoulders and drawing in the abdomen, with the *expiration* used by singers and speakers. It looks similar to Illustration B, but is used for inspiration and is fatal to satisfactory controls if used by the singer or speaker.

CHAPTER III

POSTURE AND RESPIRATION

IN the emergence of the singing voice, each set of muscular actions overlaps and blends with the next, and is responsible for both the efficiency and the freedom of the controls of the next set. This emergence, already stated in Chapter I, is that posture assists breathing, that breath control is the source of clear tones, that clear tones are a distinct help in resonation, and that full and resonant tones release the freedom of articulation. In other words, freedom in articulation is impossible without full and free resonation; a fully resonant tone is impossible without that tone being clear and breathless; flexible, clear tones are impossible without proper breath control; good breath control is impossible without an alert and active posture.

Good posture is the foundation of controlled respiration, and controlled respiration is the foundation upon which the whole voice emergence depends.

We have seen in Chapter II that adequately controlled respiration is essential to singing because of the length of phrases, the demands of crescendos and decrescendos, and of pitch precision. We must examine now the different types of breathing and find which is best suited for the controlled act of singing. The facts of how we breathe are no longer in question. The recent X-ray investigations of Bloomer[1] and the kymograph records of Shohara[2] and Card,[3] culminating a long line of research in the human breathing mechanism, give us the facts.

We breathe by expanding the cavity of the thorax (the large bony cage which protects the lungs and heart). We can expand it by lifting the chest and letting the air rush into the top of the lungs, by lifting the ribs so that the air rushes into the sides of the lungs, or by contracting and lowering the diaphragm so that the air rushes into the bottom of the lungs. These three types of breathing are sometimes called Clavicular, Intercostal, and Diaphragmatic (or Abdominal). All three overlap and blend together. No one of the three can be used without affecting the other two. The mechanism of all three can be used both for inspiration or expiration. Because we can see that at some definite

[1] Bloomer, Henry Harlan. *The Diaphragmatic Factor in Respiration.* Doctoral thesis. University of Michigan, 1933.

[2] Shohara, Hide. A temporal study in respiratory muscle actions. Research project, University of Michigan, 1946.

[3] Card, Robert E. A study of clavicular, intercostal, and diaphragmatic breathing in relationship to the control of the breath in expiration. Unpublished doctoral thesis, Detroit Institute of Musical Art, 1942.

time and place, one type is being used more strongly than the others, we have called them by separate names.

Each type of breathing has its use in daily living. *Clavicular breathing*, the rapid lifting up and down of the chest, has always been the breathing of exhaustion and anger. It is a pumping mechanism for rapidly oxidizing the blood. Done about thirty times, when not needed, one will literally acquire an oxygen "jag," become dizzy, sometimes even faint. In *expiration* it is the most powerful of the three types of breathing, its musculatures being used for expulsion, evacuation, and childbearing. It should never be used for singing purposes. All its controls are *away* from the singing mechanism instead of being directed toward it. Its natural reflex actions narrow and close the throat; cause clinical vibratos; harsh, shrill, and blatant tone qualities; and deny the singer any possibility of ever acquiring artistic flexibility in his upper range. The crude, heavy, skeletal muscles used in clavicular breathing are not built for precise and delicate controls. The prevalence of clinical vibratos in women's voices is caused by the natural tendency for many women (because of lack of physical exercise and tight clothing) to attempt to use clavicular controls for singing purposes. Bobbing heads, quivering chins, shaking throats, as well as wobbling tones, all have their source in the attempted use of large skeletal muscles for delicate controls, and most of these faults seem to emerge from clavicular breathing.

Intercostal (rib) and Diaphragmatic (abdominal) breathing should never be treated as separate types. Their overlapping and blending of muscular actions make them inseparable. The diaphragm is attached to the inside of the lower ribs, breastbone (sternum) and backbone; so diaphragm contraction must use rib action. Diaphragm contraction and rib expansion combined give the lungs their greatest *controlled* capacity.

If anyone wishes to make an examination of natural, diaphragmatic breathing for himself, probably the easiest way is for him to lie flat on his back, place his hands under the back of his head and watch the breathing process. The *abdomen* will be seen to *protrude on inspiration* and *recede on expiration*. [See Plate II.] Any movement of the chest or ribs will be negligible, the raising of the arms and hands having fully expanded the bony structure of the thorax. Thus one sees that for inspiration the contraction of the diaphragm pushes the stomach, liver, and intestines down and forward, protruding the abdominal wall. [See Plate II, Illustration A.] For expiration the resiliency of the great abdominal muscles, or their contraction, pushes the stomach, liver, and intestines back to the position they held before inspiration, while the ability of the diaphragm to resist this "abdominal lift" is the refining physiological action in the breath control of the singer.

This diaphragm descent and abdominal wall return is the action of the first breath of life, when we cry out from that undeserved spank at birth. It is the breathing we continue to use throughout life when sleeping and for quiet breathing. Shohara's investigations showed that in the unconscious breathing of 87 university students, 24 of whom were recommended soloists from the school of music, over 97% was diaphragmatic descent on inspiration and abdominal wall return on expiration.

A review of the best voice literature from the beginning of written records has shown that every great voice teacher, and all outstanding artists have used the great abdominal muscles for supporting controls while singing. The author chooses to call this action the *abdominal lift*.

From our present knowledge of physiology, let us see if we can find *why* these controls are best for singing. This involves a careful analysis of muscle action. Every great athlete carries an erect posture because an erect posture gives freedom of action to the vital organs of the body. Freedom of action to the vital organs increases vital capacity. An increased vital capacity gives greater endurance, better controls, keener efficiency in bodily actions.

In golf, tennis, baseball, football, track, basketball, swimming, and all other athletic sports we have always recognized the necessity for the study of *form*. By form we mean proper positioning of certain *large skeletal muscles* in order that the *assisting muscles* of arms and legs can make free use of the *small muscles* of flexible wrists, ankles, hands, and feet. The muscles which compose this emergent framework of muscle action are called (1) Gross Skeletal Muscles, (2) Adjunct Muscles, and (3) Minimal Motors.[4] From correct balance and overlapping and blending of these three muscle groups, emerge the keen co-ordination of our greatest athletes resulting in that beauty and ease of muscle action which make astounding athletic feats appear simple and easy. No coach ever starts a new group at an athletic sport without basing his techniques on that framework.

No intelligent piano teacher would start a student's first lesson without showing the student how posture assists arm and wrist position, and how arm and wrist position frees the use of the fingers on the keyboard. One's wildest imagination would never conceive of rigidly tightening the minimal motors of the fingers, and then hunting for the keys on the keyboard by adjustments of the gross skeletal muscles of the shoulders and body. All physiological actions, whether they are in athletics, piano playing, violin playing, or the playing of any instrument of the band or orchestra, are based on the emergence of muscular action from gross skeletal muscles through adjunct muscles to minimal motors.

[4] Muyskens, John Henry. Lecture, "Biolinguistics." University of Michigan, 1938.

Only in singing have we failed to recognize that minimal motors are released by correct emergence of gross skeletal muscle action through adjunct muscle action to the minimal motors. Only in singing have we been silly enough to think that we could correct faults by psychologically guessing from the resulting tone quality, back into the body from which it emerged.

The diaphragm is the minimal motor of breath control. The diaphragm is a thin muscular partition in the body, with the lungs and heart above and the digestive organs below. It has been humorously described as being "between the vitals and the vittles." It is fastened to the inner surface of the breastbone (sternum) in front, to the inside surface of the lower ribs all the way around the body and is anchored to the second and third lumbar vertebrae, at the small of the back, by muscular fibres. It is dome-shaped; in fact it has two domes. The stomach and spleen fit into the left dome, the liver into the right dome. At the greatest height of expiration these domes rise to the level of the fourth and fifth ribs. Examine carefully Illustrations A and B of Plate II at the beginning of this chapter; also Plate I, page 1, to become acquainted with the diaphragm action.

The diaphragm contracts and lowers. The domes are well forward in the body and the diaphragm is attached to the ribs, breastbone (sternum), and backbone at such an angle that its contraction forces the stomach, liver, and intestines not only downward but forward toward the abdominal wall. An examination of the muscles shown in Plate I, Fig. II, page 1, will show that the great abdominal muscles, by their resiliency and contraction can force the stomach, liver, and intestines against the diaphragm and force it back to its highest position, thus supporting the air of the lungs directly toward the pitch mechanism of the human larynx. *The diaphragm's contribution to breath control is in its marvelous ability of adjusting resistance to the supporting action of the great abdominal muscles.*

The diaphragm has very little sense of muscle action. One can feel the *results* of diaphragmatic action but not the action.

Embryologically (before birth), the diaphragm and the heart grow down from the neck and the diaphragm carries cervical (neck) nerves with it. It has the most precise controls of any muscle of the human body below the shoulder girdle. From these embryological facts we know that it is the minimal motor for breathing.

In spite of the fact that it has very little muscle feeling, it is under perfect *voluntary control* and responds to our slightest wish in both inspiration and expiration. In inspiration it will contract for the smallest or largest intended breath. In expiration, even if the great abdominal muscles are driving with all their power, it can, by its marvelous resistance, perfectly produce for us the most delicate pianissimo if we consciously will it to do so. By its balanced, flexible control against the adjunct muscular action of intercostal and abdominal muscles it becomes so automatic in its responses that our slightest wish in interpretation is reflected in its energy surges.

All of this precise and efficient control is possible because the whole respiratory tract is both voluntary and involuntary. Howell [5] states that "All of these muscles (of respiration) are under voluntary control. Under normal conditions, however, this entire respiratory apparatus works rhythmically without voluntary control."

This means, to the student of singing, that after he has thoroughly patterned and conditioned the voluntary acts of expiration used for singing purposes, these acts can be taken over completely by the "respiratory center" of the medulla oblongata and become involuntary. This gives the trained artist the opportunity of putting all attention on the interpretation of his text, for once conditioned to automatic use the complete act of singing becomes involuntary.

To the teacher this means the patience of Job in seeing that every student works carefully with breath controls until he has passed through the successive steps of the viability (energy), co-ordination (movement), epicritical (sensations) to interpretive (associative) level, so the student can always, at will, use perfect controls for singing, but from the standpoint of interpretation sing with a completely involuntary mechanism.

From the above descriptions it will be seen that if our breath control is to be adequate for singing purposes we must have an active, alert posture so that the gross skeletal muscles may free the adjunct muscles of ribs and abdominal wall so that the minimal motor of the diaphragm can perform with greatest ease and flexibility.

Posture is the foundation upon which the whole structure of voice emergence is built. Every individual can acquire his greatest capacity for singing and speaking by the expansion of that part of the thoracic cage which is under perfect control. This means that *an erect posture, using combined diaphragmatic and intercostal expansion for inspiration with the use of the abdominal musculatures for the supporting action of expiration, is the singer's breath.*

Many women seem to have a natural tendency to lift the chest for inspiration. A large majority of men seem to have a natural tendency to breathe diaphragmatically with very little intercostal action. To acquire a normal, natural, automatic use of the singer's breath, described above, both men and women need positive, simple techniques for its development.

All the acts of singing must be a beautiful overlapping and blending

5 Howell, William H. *Physiology,* pp. 692. Philadelphia: Saunders Co., 1942 (fourteenth edition).

of muscle action, a balanced, flexible use of the emergent musculatures of posture, respiration, phonation, resonation, and articulation.

A set military posture with chest high, shoulders back, chin in, and abdomen flat, tenses the musculatures of respiration, destroys their flexible use and defeats the purpose of posture for singing.

One foot slightly in advance of the other, weight on the balls of the feet, chest raised enough to create a firm tonic condition in the muscular actions of the ribs and abdominal wall, hands held in front, above the waist line to assist in muscular freedom, head erect but no muscles tense—in simple words, *a posture which is poised and gives a sense of being actively alert is the singer's posture.*

The posture of the boxer in the boxing ring, the posture of the batter in the batter's box, the posture of the tennis player about to serve, the posture of the golfer as he addresses his ball on the tee-off, and the posture of the vocal artist on the concert stage are all for the same purpose—*physical poise for freeing the muscle actions for the job ahead.*

Good posture is the first and basic technique in the physiological emergence of the human voice.

The second technique in the physiological emergence of the human voice is the use of the great abdominal muscles for supporting controls in expiration.

The old Hatha Yoga health science, dating back to thousands of years before the birth of Christ, had a health exercise which is applicable as a technique to assist in teaching breathing controls for singing. Turn to Plate II at the beginning of this chapter. *Without breathing,* let the abdominal muscles down as in Illustration A; then *without breathing,* literally tuck the abdomen "'way up" under the ribs as in Illustration B. *Without breathing,* do this exercise back and forth as long as you can hold your breath. A few times at first is enough to sense the supporting action of the great abdominal muscles. Do not attempt any strenuous use of this exercise at first for it would only result in lame, stiff, and sore abdominal muscles and defeat the increase of flexibility of the abdominal wall for which it should be used.

Now use the *abdominal lift* (necessary to change from Illustration A to B of Plate II) *to blow the breath out.* Almost every woman and a large percentage of men will immediately use it for inspiration instead of expiration. Practice using the *abdominal lift* for *expiration* (blowing the breath out) until it is an easy, normal, natural action to blow the breath out by lifting the abdominal muscles. We have already seen that this is normal diaphragmatic breathing by watching the breathing process while lying flat on the back.

This following through with the abdominal lift in expiration, with its full flexibility emerging from the basic technique of an active posture is the true foundation of all freedom in singing. It overlaps and blends into the free use of the pitch mechanism of the human larynx. It literally touches off reflex actions which result in an open throat for resonation. In singing, it is the source of the reflex action which causes the arching of the soft palate in the upper voice. It is the supporting action which assists the larynx as it moves up and down the throat in high and low pitches. It assists in freeing the musculatures of resonation and articulation. It gives perfect control to the end of long phrases. It is the power plant of climaxes. In expiration, it is the adjunct musculature which gives the diaphragm the chance to use its marvelous minimal motor controls. In fact, most of the faults of phonation, resonation, and articulation seem to have their source in a lack of the normal and automatic use of the abdominal lift in expiration.

From the writings of the greatest voice teachers of the past to the expressed beliefs of our present outstanding artists, we find constantly these thoughts on expiration controls:

"Do not let the ribs fall."

"Expiration is effected chiefly by the abdominal muscles."

"All breath must be supported by those strong abdominal muscles."

"The breath must be supported by the strong muscles of the abdomen."

All the weight of the empirical findings of the past; all the weight of the scientific facts of present research give us as our second technique in the emergence of the human voice, the supporting action of the great abdominal muscles for expiration. [Study carefully Plates I and II.]

Shohara [6] has recently completed an investigation, timing the muscle actions in expiration and inspiration. She has found that the normal action in *expiration* and *inspiration* is for the abdominal muscles to move first, caused by diaphragm descent on inspiration and abdominal lift on expiration.

Card's [7] investigations of clavicular, intercostal, and diaphragmatic breathing completed in 1942, show beyond any shadow of a doubt that *the resistance of the diaphragm against the energy surge of the abdominal lift is the basic technique of breath control.*

In spite of this overwhelming evidence, a large percentage of voice teachers are still driving the abdomen out with a vigorous, thrusting diaphragm descent and rigidly holding it there, while they press down upon it from above with the gross skeletal muscles of the chest and intercostals as in clavicular breathing, thus using diaphragmatic breathing for inspiration, but the crude, heavy musculatures of expulsion for

[6] Shohara, Hide. A temporal study in respiratory muscle actions. Research project, University of Michigan, 1946.

[7] Card, Robert E. A study of clavicular, intercostal, and diaphragmatic breathing in relationship to the control of the breath in expiration. Unpublished doctoral thesis, Detroit Institute of Musical Art, 1942.

expiration. The terrific force of the primitive processes of evacuation are the reverse of the beautifully balanced flexibility possible in the muscular processes of expiration. Only harsh, driven, blatant tones can possibly emerge from the use of expulsive muscular actions for breath control, and are body and tonal desecrations of the higher processes of speech and singing. Narrow, tense throats, harsh, hard tone qualities, loss of flexibility in the upper range, and clinical vibratos all arise from these inverted controls.

All of the author's research shows that the empirical findings of the past, the varying hypotheses of the great voice teachers and the theories of breath control used for hundreds of years are all pointing to a natural law of breath control for singing, in which the gross skeletal muscles of posture assist the adjunct muscles of the abdominal wall to free the minimal motor controls of the diaphragm, and that:

The abdominal lift, initiating the energy surge in expiration, with the diaphragm resistance controlling the pressure at the vocal lips, is the second basic technique in the physiological emergence of the human voice.

The flexibility of the abdominal lift has a complete range from the precise balanced setting of its musculatures for pianissimo humming to the buoyant welling up of the powerful energy surges necessary for sforzando attacks or fortissimo climaxes. From this it will be seen that one should always remember that the basic truth of the use of the abdominal lift is that it is exactly in proportion to the task at hand, for it is the energy surge against which the diaphragm resistance actually controls the breath.

This brings us to six definite and positive physiological techniques for the development of a breath control adequate for artistic interpretation in singing.

First: Stand or sit erect, with a poise which is actively alert.

Second: The action of expansion for inspiration is in exact proportion to the intention of the singer in the length and power of the phrase to be sung.

Third: Breathe noiselessly through the nose and mouth.

Fourth: Use diaphragmatic breathing so that the controlling muscles may have free play in their work.

Fifth: Balance the breath against the resistance of the closed vocal lips that the tone produced may be breathless and not forced.

Sixth: Follow through to the end of the phrase with the supporting action of the abdominal lift.

The following paragraph has been left to the end of the chapter to emphasize more thoroughly the use of the abdominal lift and to explain its elusive controls.

Too much rib expansion flattens the diaphragm without the necessity of the diaphragm contracting, thus destroying the flexibility of the diaphragm descent and abdominal lift. This shows that for control purposes, diaphragm descent is more important than intercostal expansion and should be evident through **abdominal protrusion before rib expansion occurs.** *When the tone is clear,* the initial attack of the abdominal lift and diaphragm resistance builds up the breath pressure at the vocal lips and one feels a sense of buoyant support from the abdominal wall. The lift then seems to suspend its action and continues to lift with imperceptible support, except for the vigorous additional lifts for *emphasis, power, height of melodic line,* or *end of phrase.* *When the tone produced is breathy,* the initial attack never suspends and the abdominal wall continues to lift so rapidly that all breath is expelled in such a short time that one has the feeling of the abdominal wall literally "caving in" quickly with complete loss of breath. The physiological fact that both vocal lips and diaphragm have very little kinesthetic sense (muscle action sense), makes the understanding of this action of support and suspension of the abdominal lift (because of diaphragm and vocal lip resistance) of utmost importance in the development of automatic and efficient breath control. The abdominal lift must follow through with a steady continuous support to the end of every phrase with special energy surges for climaxes, careful support for low tones; in fact it is the only source of breath pressure in artistic singing and never ceases to function for even a fraction of a second in any phrase without disastrous results to the beauty of tone. *In artistic singing the abdominal lift builds the crude breath pressure which the diaphragm refines for the emergence of beautiful tone.* Just as in every muscle action of the human body the resisting muscle delivers the controls, so the resistance of the diaphragm to the abdominal lift delivers breath control to the vocal lips.

One of the most important phases of rhythmic spacing of breath control is the abdominal lifts on long phrases. The average person can use four energy surges from the abdominal wall in the rhythmic pattern of a single phrase. Some can use only three, some have five. These lifts must be spaced rhythmically for economy in long phrases. In over forty years of listening to "Messiah" concerts the writer has yet to hear a nationally known oratorio singer sing the "high mountain" phrase in "O Thou That Tellest Glad Tidings to Zion" in one breath. Any normal singer can do it with perfect ease, and have breath left, if the above rhythmic spacing of abdominal lifts is observed.

To check oneself for diaphragmatic breathing, one should always be certain that on both inspiration and expiration the abdominal wall moves first. In *inspiration* the secondary action is in the expansion of the ribs and in *expiration* the secondary action is in the contraction of the ribs. The visual primary action in inspiration is the expansion of the abdominal wall and primary action in expiration is in the contraction of the abdominal wall. This primary expansion of the abdominal wall upon inspiration is caused by the diaphragm descent. This descent of the diaphragm forces the liver into the *soft triangle* between the floating ribs, distending the abdominal wall. *A warning must be given that this place of expansion is not the same in different individuals, varying as much as five inches up and down the trunk according to body build.* In some "long-waisted" individuals the "soft-triangle," referred to above, is below the belt line. In expiration, the contraction of the abdominal wall starts to flatten this distension. As the abdominal lift continues, the abdomen is literally "tucked up" under the ribs as the lift builds the breath pressure which the diaphragm resists in its ascent to its original lax position. For the best control of the breath, in both singing and speaking, the abdominal wall should move first, both in inspiration and expiration.

INSTRUCTIONS FOR PLATE III

Figure A. A frontal section of the vocal lips and trachea to show the process of
phonation.
    EP.—epiglottis in stipple to indicate that the section is made looking
from the back toward the tongue down the flat edges of the vocal
lips which are closed as in singing a clear tone.
    Th.C.—thyroid cartilage.
    F.V.C.—false vocal cords.
    V.L.—vocal ligament.
    M.V.L.—muscles of the vocal lip.
    C.E.—conus elasticus.
    C.C.—cricoid cartilage.
    T.—trachea.

Figure B. Horizontal section through the vocal lips showing deep breathing.
    Th.C.—thyroid cartilage.
    V.L.—vocal ligament.
    A.C.—arytenoid cartilage.

Figure C. Quiet breathing.

Figure D. Breathy tone.

Figure E. Clear tone—low pitch.

Figure F. Clear tone—medium pitch.

Figure G. Clear tone—high pitch and mezza-voce.

Figure H. Falsetto.

PLATE III

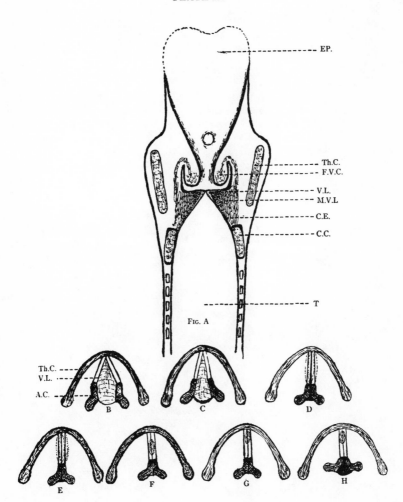

FIG. A

EP.
Th.C.
F.V.C.
V.L.
M.V.L
C.E.
C.C.
T

Th.C.
V.L.
A.C.

B   C   D

E   F   G   H

Chapter IV

PHONATION

THE valve at the top of the trachea (windpipe), known as the larynx (Adam's apple), was developed for a single purpose—to protect the lungs from foreign bodies. Its many cartilages, ligaments, muscles, and nerves have grown to be efficient in that work. The vocal lips can close for that purpose. The arytenoid cartilages to which the vocal ligaments (vocal cords) are attached in back, can be approximated to occlusion and folded in tight to the epiglottis for that purpose. The whole larynx can be lifted and the root of the tongue pulled back over it for that purpose. This three-way valve makes it very difficult for any foreign matter to enter the lungs.

Nearly all the animal kingdom uses this breathing valve in the throat, for making sounds. This is a simple modification from its original purpose, for when it is not closed too tightly, breath pressure from below forces the vocal lips to open in an explosive puff which causes a vibration in the air column above and below the vocal lips. The vocal lips are so resilient in their action that they return to their closed position quickly only to spring open again by the pressure from below. A pitch of a' in modern tuning has 440 of these puffs per second. (A similar action in sound production to that of the vocal lips, is the vibration of the brass instrument player's lips in the mouthpiece of his instrument. That this is the action of the vocal lips is shown objectively by the marvelous pictures made recently in the Bell Telephone Laboratories of the vocal lips during phonation.)

The necessary investigation of the manner in which the vocal lips produce their vibrations throughout the range of the human voice has been a matter of research from the time of the invention of the laryngoscope by Manuel Garcia to the recent histological investigations reported by Strong[1] in 1935, and still continuing at the Chicago Medical School. Strong examined, with the microscope, cross sections of the false and true vocal lips, made in 1/2500 of an inch in thickness. All the tissues (folds, ligaments, muscles, and nerves) were examined in order to determine their function. The author has spent many hours examining Strong's slides through the microscope. Study thoroughly and carefully the Illustrations of Plate III at the beginning of this chapter. Illustrations B, C, D, E, F, G, and H show the actions of the vocal lips in breathing and singing.

[1] Strong, Leon Henri. "The Mechanism of Laryngeal Pitch," *Anatomical Record*, LXIII, No. 1 (August 25, 1935).

Investigation in this field has found answers to questions of registration, falsetto, fundamental and overtone resonation and vowel action; through Strong's investigations, those of the Bell Telephone Laboratories, and those of the author, following the ground work of the past, culminating with Muyskens' thesis on "The Hypha"[2] and Hide Shohara's in the "Genesis of the Articulatory Movements."[3] The results of these investigations are given fully in the present chapter and the chapters on *Resonation, Humming, Articulation,* and *Vibrato.*

Illustration A of Plate III, at the beginning of this chapter, with its frontal section of the larynx, shows the epiglottis (in stipple), ventricular folds (false vocal cords), vocal lips (with fold, ligament and muscle fibres), thyroid and cricoid cartilages, conus elasticus and tracheal sections. This illustration gives a clear picture of how the breath pressure from below being concentrated at the glottal edges (contact point of vocal lips) through the shape of the conus elasticus (elastic cone at the top of the windpipe) causes the puffs of air to escape, which by the condensation and rarefaction of the air column produce what are known as sound vibrations.

These vibrations in the air column must never be confused with the breath or air itself. If an individual blows with all the power of his abdominal lift, the actual breath will only travel a few feet. The sound waves produced by the puffs at the vocal lips travel at the rate of nearly 1300 feet a second, at body temperature. *When these puffs are made from closed vocal lips the cleanness of the resulting vibration impinges on the ear drum of the human ear with a distinctness which we recognize as a clear tone.* [See Illustration E of Plate III.] When the vocal lips are slightly separated and more breath escapes than is necessary for the production of the puffs, we recognize the resulting tone as a weak, lifeless, breathy tone. [See Illustration D of Plate III.]

Artistic singing is in the production of clear tones. Enrico Caruso, probably the greatest voice the world has yet heard, stated that he spent his whole life developing a maximum of resonance with a minimum of breath.

The vocal ligaments have no conscious feeling of muscle action. The diaphragm has very little feeling of muscle action (kinesthetic sensation). These two physiological facts make the production of breathless tone vibrations a very elusive accomplishment.

This does not mean that the diaphragm and vocal lips are involuntary. They are used as voluntarily as any muscles of the human body,

[2] Muyskens, John Henry. *The Hypha.* Doctoral dissertation, University of Michigan, 1925.

[3] Shohara, Hide Helen. *Genesis of the Articulatory Movements of Speech with Special Reference to the Processes of Sucking, Chewing, and Swallowing.* Doctoral dissertation, University of Michigan, 1932.

responding to the slightest wish of the individual as he speaks or sings. Under training they become automatic in their action and the fact that they have no conscious feeling of muscle action makes them extremely flexible instruments for use in interpretation. How then can the body be trained in the balanced, flexible use of abdominal lift, diaphragm action and clean, breathless puffs of the vocal lips? By the use of normal reflex actions which are patterned and conditioned by lifetime use in the human body. To sort out those reflex actions, to build and modify them for more artistic speech and singing, is the true task of the vocal teacher and student.

To understand the elusive preciseness of that task, one should know how the varying speeds of puffs are produced by the vocal lips, for all the hypotheses and theories of past vocal training are based on beliefs concerning the functioning of the vocal lips.

Strong's investigations and all the pictures made of the vocal lips in action show that the vocal folds vibrate in full length of glottal edges for low tones (Illust. E, Plate III), in a varying central segment for medium range (Illust. F, Plate III), and in varying small segments, well forward on the vocal lips, for extremely high tones and falsetto (Illusts. G and H, Plate III). (The author would prefer to designate *tones* and *pitches*, which are merely hearing perceptions, as *vibrations* and use the terms *slow* and *fast*, but usage makes *low pitches, medium pitches*, and *high pitches* more understandable to the average reader.)

These different types of vibrations have produced a vast amount of theoretical teaching of so-called "registers" in the human voice which will be treated thoroughly in the chapter on *Resonation* when dealing with fundamental and overtone resonation.

Strong's work shows that the mechanism for pitch adjustment in the vocal lips is a microscopic interweaving of muscle fibres in and out of the vocal ligament giving the power of adjustment within the glottal edge itself. Just as the well developed embouchure of the brass instrument player has a flexibility of seven overtones merely by increase of breath pressure and tension, so the marvelous adjustments within the glottal edges of the vocal lips have developed a microscopic muscle control for minute changes of pitch throughout the range of the human voice. For many years the medical profession has known that the use of the large powerful muscles in the vocal lips are for pulling the arytenoid cartilages forward to the epiglottis to close the upper end of the larynx during the act of swallowing.

The precise mechanism described above gives perfect adjustment for the slightest variation of vibration length and speeds within the entire range of the human voice, and answers all questions of the "how" of that adjustment. For greater power, tension of the larger muscles (balanced antagonism of the thyro-arytenoids and thyro-cricoids) add to the volume of resistance at the vocal lips. Illustrations E, F, G, and H of Plate III show the types of varying innervations used in pitch adjustments of the glottal edges. Illustration H of the falsetto tone, showing the opening of the cartilages for breath escape at the same time the tone vibrations are being produced in the forward segment of the vocal lips, has been known since the investigations of Thomas French in 1891 and beautifully illustrated by the Bell Telephone pictures of 1939 and those following. The difference between true mezza-voce and falsetto are clearly shown in Illustrations G and H, the mezza-voce being with the vocal lips closed throughout their entire length. The so-called "break" in the attempted crescendo of a falsetto tone is caused by the necessity of closing the vocal lips. A true mezza-voce crescendos without a "break."

Old theories of the vocal cords stretching and shortening in their own intrinsic length by the large muscle actions of the larynx must take their place with other discarded beliefs, as the equipment for investigation advances.

This now known fact of precise adjustment within the glottal edges themselves fits all the pictures made, and the views seen with the laryngoscope, from the beginning of the work of Manuel Garcia to the high speed camera pictures of the Bell Telephone Laboratories, and gives a new and lasting concept of the mechanism of this breathing valve at the top of the windpipe, and must not be confused with the crescendo and decrescendo mechanism of thinning and thickening of the glottal edges through light and strong closure pressures at any pitch.

All of the above description is given merely to impress upon the mind of both student and teacher that:

First: The vocal lips are capable of producing clear or breathy tones.

Second: The vocal lips can adjust themselves for fast and slow vibrations of varying power.

Third: The vocal lips have no conscious sense of feeling.

Then how can one learn to sing clearly?

The author has reviewed all available voice literature from the beginning of the publication of voice textbooks and has found no definite technique of any kind for clear tone production. It is true, he did find many attempted descriptions of the sensation of clear tone production, such as the one sighted in the chapter on *Respiration*, "Do not let the ribs fall," also "Start the tone on the suspension of the breath" (silly,

for tone can only start with breath pressure), "Feel as if you drew
your breath in as you start the tone instead of blowing it out" (no
comment necessary), "Use a light cough to make yourself conscious of
the glottal action" (entirely false, for the glottal edges are without conscious muscle sensation), and innumerable others, all bearing on the
subject in hazy, psychological ways, but none of them techniques for a
clear tone or its development.

There is however a very definite technique for developing clear tone
production. It comes from a normal reflex action used by practically
the whole English speaking peoples. It is the use of the spoken, colloquial, closed-lip affirmative, *m-hm*. The author has yet to find, after
more than forty years of teaching, the pupil who pronounces a breathy *m*
in the first half of *m-hm*. Produced exactly as when spoken and prolonged into an *m*-hum, the initial *m* of *m-hm* becomes a positive technique for sensing the production of clear tone.

One notices immediately two definite things for judging the clear
hum. First, the abdominal lift builds up the necessary pressure for the
clear hum and then seems to suspend its lifting action. This seeming
suspension is caused by the fact that a clear tone uses so little breath
in its production that the lift of the abdominal wall becomes imperceptible after the pressure is built. Second, the feeling created by the
transmission of the tone vibrations into the bony structure of the head
is one of firmness, as if the vibrations remained in the head above the
level of the roof of the mouth.

With the breathy hum, the abdominal lift, instead of building pressure, "caves in," for the breath is used up as fast as it can be supplied.
The breathy hum also has a second means of identification, for the
breath and tone vibrations seem to flow out of the nostrils and are not
retained in the bony structure of the head.

The author's recent work has shown that the *m*-hum, produced
without muscle interference in either the pharynx, muscles of the soft
palate, or tongue, produces strong reinforcement of fundamental tone
and is the basis of development of both clear tones and free resonation.
The chapter on *Humming* thoroughly describes this basic technique and
its use.

The third basic technique in the emergence of the human
voice is the development of the ability to sing with closed vocal
lips for the production of clear tone.

There has been an enormous amount of discussion about what type
of musical instrument the human voice is. To the author this seems to
be a rather inane, fruitless controversy, for the pitch mechanism of the
human body has elements of practically all musical instruments yet
developed by man. The vocal lips vibrate in varying lengths and segments similar to string instruments. They produce sound waves by

condensation and rarification of the air by puffs like a player's lips in the mouthpiece of a brass instrument. They vibrate against each other in a sort of reverse setup of the double reeds of the reed instrument family. They use the air column above them similar to organ pipes. They use the bronchial tubes and chest like a mixed bassoon and bass violin. They use the pharynx, naso-pharynx, nose and mouth as coupled resonators. They transmit their vibrations through muscles, membranes, tissues, and ligaments to the whole bony structure of the upper part of the body—chest, shoulder girdle, vertebral column, sinuses and all the bone structure of the head, like a piano soundboard, violin box, etc. In fact, the human voice is the most complicated, yet simplest and precise musical instrument the world has ever seen. The problem of the voice scientist is to find simple techniques by which the musculatures involved in the production of tone can so perfectly overlap and blend and balance against one another that practically every action involved in the singing act can be so effortless that it remains at or near the level of the tonic condition of good posture. Only the power plant musculatures of the abdominal lift and the resistance musculatures of the suspension and intrinsic actions of the larynx need to rise above that level.

PLATE IV.
RESONATION

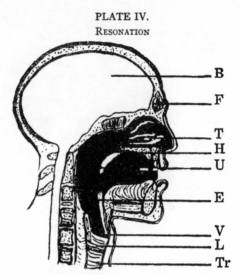

B
F
T
H
U
E
V
L
Tr

A diagram of a median section through the head showing the cavities and bony structures in which and through which the tone vibrations are resonated and transmitted until the complete cavity and bony structure reverberate with the phenomenon known as resonation. B—Brain cavity; F—Frontal sinus; T—Turbinate bones; H—Hard palate; U—Uvula; E—Epiglottis; V—Vocal cords; L—Larynx; Tr—Trachea.

SOLID BLACK—The HUMAN RESONATOR AND TRANSMITTER, should be used as a single unit, with the upper half re-enforcing the fundamental tone and the lower half re-enforcing the vowel forms with such freedom of muscle action that the vibrations are transmitted freely into the bony structures for full resonation. When the muscle actions of the resonation are used freely the tones produced are always beautiful, but when tensions occur in any musculatures of phonation, resonation or articulation the tone loses its beauty and becomes mouthy, nosey or throaty according to the place of distortion.

PLATE V.
THE NASAL SCROLLS

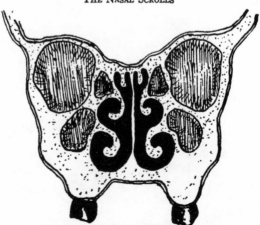

A Transverse Section of the Human Face.

CHAPTER V

RESONATION

WHEN tone vibrations are produced they travel in every direction from their source. They are not restricted to air but can travel in any material having mass and elasticity. They rebound from hard surfaces but are absorbed or transmitted in certain kinds of material.

The study of the laws of sound is a branch of the science of Physics and is called acoustics or sonics. It is, by some, divided into two types of research: catacoustics, the study of reflected sound, and diacoustics, the study of sound transmitted directly to the ear from sonorous bodies. If a cavity or material in which the tone is vibrating, is of the right size and shape, this ability to rebound, or vibrate in phase, increases the tone enormously in volume. The term, *Resonance,* is used in physics and related fields to describe the prolongation or increase of sound due to sympathetic vibration of some cavity or body capable of moving in proper period.

The term, *Resonation,* is a comparatively new term. The voice teaching profession has known so little concerning the muscular acts by which the tone becomes more fully resonated, that until recently, the static term, *resonance,* has been sufficient. As respiration, inspiration, expiration, phonation, and articulation are all terms of muscular activity, so *resonation* is the only term to express the muscular activity by which the tones produced by the pitch mechanism of the human larynx become resonated.

The act of resonation permits great power of sound to develop from a comparatively weak source. Inversely, the act of resonation relieves strain and effort at the source of the vibrations.

Much of the research work in acoustics has been done with cavities and hard surfaces for the study of resonance in buildings, organ pipes, and musical instruments; or with porous absorbing surfaces for eradicating reverberations. The telephone and radio opened a whole new field of sound investigation in membranous and electrical transmission.

As far as the author knows, the only investigation into the laws of sound as they apply to live tissue covered with mucous, and in the living structures of the human body, is one by the author in 1939 and reinstated in 1954, with the assistance of Wilmer Bartholomew[1] and

---

[1] Bartholomew, Wilmer T. *Acoustics of Music.* Prentice Hall, 1946.

Gordon Peterson[2] at the Speech Laboratories of the University of Michigan. This research is still in its preliminary stage. Two bone conduction microphones were connected with an oscilloscope. The author produced a pianissimo *m*-hum. The oscilloscope reported only fundamental
tone; from the top of the head, the forehead, the temporal bones, the
mastoid bones, the sides of the nose, the upper and lower jaw, the upper
vertebral column, the shoulder blades, the breast bone, and the collar
bone. Any hum with muscle interference in the walls of the throat was
not transmitted through the structures to the bone conduction microphones, except on the sides of the larynx itself.

To the student of voice, as a producer of tone, the resonation of the
human voice is not the study of catacoustics with its emphasis on reflected sound from hard surfaced resonance chambers, nor is it even the
study of diacoustics with its medium the transmission of sound through
moisture-filled, mucous-lined cavities, live tissues and bones of the
human body.

To the student of voice, the study of resonation in the human voice
is the study of techniques by which the normal reflex actions of the
body (bearing on the muscle actions of larynx, pharynx, nasopharynx,
soft palate, jaw, tongue, and lips) will allow the tone vibrations produced by the vocal lips to seek all available resonance in the human
body with the least possible interference. Bartholomew states that all
of the findings of his fifteen years of research in acoustics would point
to the fact that the muscular position of the pianissimo *m*-hum, as
described in the chapter on humming, is a perfect muscular setting for
freedom of resonation in singing. It may take several years of research
on many subjects and new equipment to find all the facts in the transmission of sound through tissues, bones, and cavities of the human
body. Still to the teacher and student the significance of the muscle
actions of a pianissimo *m*-hum being a basic physiological approach to
resonation is invaluable. [To become acquainted with the construction
of the pharynx (throat), nasopharynx (cavity above the soft palate
behind the nose), nose, and mouth, examine thoroughly and carefully
the illustrations of Plates I, IV, and V. These are purely schematic but
will give the student a clear concept of the relationship of the cavities
and structures involved in the resonation of the human voice.]

If we are to have any true concepts of the worth of certain techniques in voice training we must make an analysis of the facts of
resonation as we know them today.

We have already seen in Chapter IV that the explosive puffs of the
vocal lips produce the condensation and rarefaction of the air column
which we call sound waves. We know from the sound investigations of

2 Peterson, Gordon, Director of Speech Laboratories, University of Michigan.

numerous physicists and sound engineers that vowels are resonant reinforcements of certain bands of frequency (vowel formants) either fixed or relative to the pitch on which the vowel is sung or spoken. If we examine the results of these investigations we find that the rates of vibrations of these vowel frequency bands vary enormously. On the $\overline{oo}$ (as in *to*) vowel, they have ranged all the way from König's 244 vibrations per second to Boeke's 588. On the $\bar{e}$ (as in *he*) vowel, the variation is from Donder's 1381 per second to König's 3906. Two of our best known American physicists and sound engineers strike a happy medium with D. C. Miller's $\overline{oo}$ at 362 and $\bar{e}$ with a high rate of 3100 and I. B. Crandall's $\overline{oo}$ at 407 and $\bar{e}$ at 2435. Recent research allots to most vowels at least two rates of vibrations, a lower and a higher, varying in energy according to the vowel.

If these vowel formants (rates of vibrations) were of primary importance in the resonation of the human voice and were actually at definite rates, we could devise a scale of vowels, matching pitches with vowel vibration rates through care in selection of fundamental tones from which the vowel frequencies were easily derived as upper partials and then say to the student of voice, "This is the vowel scale. By using this we can make singing easy for you." This is being attempted by some voice teachers.

The flaws in such a hypothesis are readily seen. First, the vowel frequencies listed above show that vowels are not at definite rates, unless sung or spoken with identical "color." [In the chapter on *Articulation*, techniques for making vowels uniform are discussed.] The rates of the $\overline{oo}$ vowel vary by more than an octave, being found by different investigators at 244, 294, 325, 345, 362, 383, 392, 407, and 588 vibrations per second, and in the $\bar{e}$ vowel, the band of frequency covers such a wide range of fast vibrations that practically any pitch sung by the human voice would have upper partials within that frequency band. Second, the author's recent investigations have shown that in any voice of recognized merit, the fundamental tone on which the vowel is sung is more powerfully resonated than the vowel formant.

The two statements above coupled with the very self-evident fact that all great artists sing with a uniform resonance on all vowels at all pitches (except that $\bar{e}$ as in *he*, and $\overline{oo}$ as in *to*, sometimes become modified to i as in *sit*, and $o\breve{o}$ as in *look*, at high pitches through their interference with resonation musculatures) show that any hypothesis of a vowel formant scale technique for voice training purposes, is false.

The fully resonated tone, recognized in perception as rich, dark, vibrant, thrilling, round, full, or whatever one wishes psychologically to call the tone quality of a beautiful voice, is strong in fundamental resonation. The harsh, shrill, blatant, screamy, white, knifey, piercing tone which tortures the nervous system is strong in vowel formant resonation.

Any vocal teacher is perfectly welcome to ruin his professional career by trying to develop voices through emphasis on vowel formant exercises but if he wishes to develop beautiful voices he had better search for techniques in the strengthening of fundamental resonation and through that strength develop a uniformity of resonant quality on all vowels, which will build what the great voice teachers of the past have called a "uniform resonant line." The simplest way to express this to the student is "a uniform amount of hum in the voice."

NASALIZATION AND ORALIZATION

Finding that in voices of recognized beauty the fundamental tone received the strongest resonation, the writer made an investigation of the fundamental and overtones to determine where they received their reinforcement. With a specially-designed oscillograph and high speed camera, the effect of nasalization and oralization was studied in the wave form.

There was overwhelming evidence in every subject examined that nasalization *increased the strength of fundamental tone resonance and that* oralization *increased the strength of vowel formant resonance.* In perception, increase in strength of fundamental was increase in beauty of tone quality, while increase in strength of vowel formant was increase in disagreeable harshness. The greatest beauty of tone quality was always accompanied by what the subject experienced as the greatest freedom from muscle interference and a resonation feel of tone vibrations in the bony structure of the head, in the pharynx, nasopharynx, and nose, as well as mouth. The muscular action involved in vowel formation in such tone production was so free that it was without sense of feeling.

NASAL PORT CLOSURES

Every time we swallow we close the nasal port (the soft palate doorway into the nasopharynx and nose) to keep food from going into the nasal passages. If we regurgitate we close the port for the same reason. The reflex action of gagging closes the nasal port. In speaking and singing, all consonantal actions, except *m, n,* and *ng* close the nasal port. (In some exceptionally beautiful singing and speaking voices, the nasal port remains open on *l* and *r*.)

We have seen above, that strength of resonance in the fundamental tone is necessary to beauty in voice emergence and that increase in resonance of fundamental tone is acquired through resonation above the level of the soft palate. This means that the development of beauty in singing is not only through an open throat and freedom in articulation but is also in proportion to the freedom with which the open nasal port is used and the tone vibrations transmitted into the structures above the level of the roof of the mouth.

This is true not only for singing but for speech. Recent investigations at the speech clinic at the University of Michigan have shown that public speakers of recognized, exceptional worth, use an open nasal port on all vowels. It is necessary then that we recognize as voice training techniques all of those normal reflex actions which assist in forming habits of opening the nasal port. The essential techniques for resonation are those techniques which will assist in developing an open throat and in developing, in the upper part of the range, the arching of the soft palate with the nasal port open.

NASAL PORT OPENINGS AND ARCHINGS

Breathing through the nose, or nose and mouth combined, the *m*, *n*, and *ng* hums, and yawning, all use an open nasal port, while the reflex actions of swallowing and regurgitating assist in the arching of the soft palate and opening of the throat but close the nasal port.

The arching and lowering of the soft palate in ascending and descending scales, with the nasal port open throughout the range, *is the secret of uniform resonation, tone quality and the blending of pitch mechanism changes.*

This arching and lowering of the soft palate for high and low pitches apparently has a two-fold significance. In the first place it is part of the balanced control in the normal raising and lowering of the larynx during the production of high and low pitches. And second, it seems to have real significance in the resonation of the fundamental tone by directing the tone vibration transmission of the higher pitches toward the smaller cavities above the level of the roof of the mouth. The X-ray investigations of Secord[3] at the University of Michigan, completed in April 1941, shows that any fixed position of the larynx, either high or low, is a false concept in voice teaching, for its natural action is to rise on high pitches and lower on low pitches. It would seem that this natural tendency is responsible (because of the slight muscle feel which attends it) for practically all beginning students thinking pitches as high and low and attempting to assist the muscle actions by "reaching for high tones." Of course such attempts are senseless, for the breath pressure from the abdominal lift takes care of the actions in the throat, and any looking up, raising the head, thrusting up with the chin, or any other tensions about the head, neck, or throat only

---

3 Secord, Arthur E. *An X-ray Study of the Hyoid Bone, Thyroid Cartilage, and the Cricoid Cartilage in Relation to Pitch Change in the Human Larynx.* Doctoral thesis, University of Michigan, April 1941.

hinder the normal actions. The old Italian empirical finding of "when you sing up, sing down" is sound advice, for it has a tendency to leave the larynx free to move up and down the throat without interference. The muscular actions for arching and lowering of the soft palate are thoroughly discussed in the chapter on *Humming*.

REGISTERS

The subject of registers in the human voice has been left by the author until the details of the overlapping and blending of abdominal lift, clear tone production, and nasal port opening have been thoroughly described, for in this balanced flexible emergence of the muscular activities of posture, respiration, phonation, and resonation lies the eradication of register difficulties.

In the chapter on *Phonation* we explained the three shifts of pitch mechanism for low range, medium range, and high range tones. [Plate III, Illust. E, F, G.] If the tone vibrations are over-oralized, these shifts, with their attendant muscular actions (attempting to align the muscles for proper resonation), become very prominent and are called *registers*. Because of the seeming location of these oralized tone vibrations (in perception) they have been designated as chest, medium, and head registers.

To protect the throat from the strain caused by this oralization, generally the vocal lips give way in the upper voice, and women's voices shift to breathy tones, while men's voices change to falsetto. If the muscular strength of the individual throat is able to stand the strain, the upper voice will become hard, white, shrill, or throaty, but the vocal lips will hold.

This shrillness, caused by tensions of oralized voice emergence, must not be confused with the thrilling ring of all high voices freely produced. Bartholomew's research shows that this ringing quality seems to be the fast vibrations of the resonation of the cavity just above the vocal lips in the larynx itself.

Manuel Garcia noticed many years ago that well "rounded" tones tended to bridge these gaps. As has been previously stated in this chapter, we now know that darker tones (well "rounded" tones) are exactly in proportion to the amount of resonation above the soft palate, caused by the use of the open nasal port. Registers disappear exactly in proportion to the balanced, flexible co-ordination of abdominal lift, clear tones, and open nasal port. The reason for this is the law of resonance stated at the beginning of this chapter: "The act of resonation relieves strain and effort at the source of the vibrations." The fuller resonation caused by the use of the nasopharynx and nose through the open nasal port allows the pitch mechanism of the vocal lips and the raising and lowering of the larynx to perform their adjustments with such ease that the so-called registers cease to exist.

One of the biggest surprises in the author's recent investigations in nasalization and oralization was the discovery that the quality always described as "nasal twang" *is not caused by too much use of the nose but because the nose is blocked.* Blocking can be done by any one of five different nasal obstructions: closure at the nostrils; a cold; deformed turbinates; adenoids; or a partial nasal port closure through the *ng* position at the back of the tongue. Any one or all five of these may cause the quality called the "nasal twang." (The nasal twang of the cleft palate patient comes under the first category, for it is caused by the nostrils being too small to allow the free passage of the abnormal number of tone vibrations resulting from the use of the enormous nasal spaces.) *Nasalization* through an open nasal port when the passages through the nasopharynx and nose are free, *never results in a "nasal twang" but is the technique for its cure.*

With beginning voice students, the register prominence caused by oralized singing has a certain doubtful worth to the voice teacher, for in low altos and basses the break between the middle and upper range generally falls between A and B♭ or B♭ and B♮, while in mezzos and baritones it appears between C and C♯ or C♯ and D, and in sopranos and tenors between E♭ and E♮ or E♮ and F, thus giving to both teacher and student an estimate in the first lesson of what the voice may be when developed. We said of "doubtful worth" because in many beginning students it will already be above its natural position as it shifts upward when nasalization (resonation above the soft palate through the open nasal port) is sufficient to relieve some of the strain on the pitch mechanism. Because of this upward shift when oralization is not too prominent, some altos might be thought mezzos or mezzos judged as sopranos, or baritones as tenors. The safest and best teaching, totally ignores registers and allows the *tessitura* (that part of the range in which one sings the easiest) to develop in each individual naturally through correct techniques of posture, respiration, phonation, resonation, and articulation. Through this positive physiological approach, the voice seeks its own natural range, which sometimes extends to over three octaves, and develops a natural tendency toward greater freedom in a high, low, or medium tessitura.

We have seen in the chapters on *Respiration* and *Phonation* that the action of the abdominal lift assists in the positioning of the pitch mechanism in clear tone production and resonation actions. We have now seen that the abdominal lift, clear tone production, and resonation actions assist the balance of fundamental and overtone resonation from which beauty of tone in vowel production emerges.

In both clear tone production and resonation, basic techniques have pointed toward the *m*-hum.

We must not leave our thinking of resonation without a full realization of the fact that all the tissues of the human body, except the bones, are largely water and that water transmits sound better than air. If we are to think correctly of the resonation of the human voice, we must stop thinking of cavity resonance only. We must realize that the pharynx, nasopharynx, nose and mouth are not only resonance cavities re-enforcing fundamental tones and vowel forms, but are also transmitters of tone vibrations to the complete bony structure of the upper body and head.

Such localized expressions as "singing in the mask" or "pharyngeal resonance" should only be used by the voice teaching profession to describe faults. If a light lyric soprano had been trained for years with an *n*-hum as a basic technique until practically all the tone she produced was vibrating in the confined localization of a high frontal resonance, one might be justified in telling her she was "singing in the mask." Or, on the other hand, if through downward breathing pressures the throat had been narrowed, and then the teacher, by local emphasis on an "open throat," had forced the student into the use of throat muscle tensions, and the resulting hard surfaced pharyngeal cavity showed in the quality of "pharyngeal resonance," one would be justified in so naming it.

The use of the terms *nasalization, oralization,* and *full resonation* indicates to the student accurately what cavities he is using and keeps his attention on the free transmission of all tone vibrations *into the cavities* and *through the tissues* to the bony framework of all the resonating structures of the human body and gives to him the ideal of the ultimate goal of the firm sureness of a fully resonated voice.

We will close our *Resonation* discussion with this simple statement:

The fourth basic technique for the emergence of the human voice is the development of strong fundamental tone resonance, through the patterning and conditioning of the coordinated use of the abdominal lift, a clear tone, and an open nasal port.

PLATE VI.

HARD PALATE ARCH FORMS

Front View   Side View

 I

 II

 III

 IV

CHAPTER VI

ARTICULATION

ARTICULATION is the most complicated of the five steps in the emergence of the human voice. Voice teachers have used the term *diction*, until it has become a synonym for enunciation and articulation. *Articulation* is concerned with "vocal movements." *Diction* is primarily a term having for its basic meaning "the choice of words for the expression of ideas." In vocal music, *diction* is already set by the author and composer. *Articulation* is distinctly a problem of the student as a producer.

Through constant practice in earliest childhood, each normal individual finally develops the ability to pronounce the sounds used by his elders. He makes the necessary adjustments of lips, tongue, soft palate, jaw, and throat to compensate for variations in shapes of lips, teeth, cheeks, tongue, hard palate, soft palate, nose, nasopharynx, throat, larynx, etc., in order to imitate accurately the sounds he hears. These actions finally become automatic and remain as lifetime habits.

It is hard for most of us to realize that in singing and speech, we are not dealing with letters or even sounds but with the muscular actions which produce those sounds. A small glimpse at some odd spellings, all of which use the same muscle actions resulting in the sound *ō* such as *oats, sew, dough, foe, crow, beau,* and then another glimpse of the letter *o* with such odd sounds as in *obey, go, odd, not, nothing, order, foot,* and *food,* and one will see the futility of thinking either in letters or sounds in English. Muscular actions and their resulting sounds are the only true basis for the study of speech and singing. It would pay big dividends in a true understanding of voice problems, if all voice teachers would spend a year or two, as the author did, in teaching totally deaf people to articulate distinctly.

The only modification from cultured speech necessary for artistic singing is that the vowels must be pure. For in the speed of speech they are constantly made impure by the overlapping and blending of the preceding and succeeding consonants. This necessitates greater accuracy and speed in the articulation of consonants in singing as compared with speech. It also demands greater care in the purity of vowel forms. Review Chapter II.

When resonation of the fundamental tone is full and free, articulation becomes easy. When the muscular activities of resonation are not fully developed, some articulatory movements are very difficult to make because of the interference of the poorly produced resonation actions.

Neither the teacher nor student must ever lose sight of the framework of voice emergence. In that framework of posture, respiration, phonation, resonation, and articulation, all the way from the large skeletal muscles of posture through to the most precise action of the tip of the tongue in articulation, all musculatures are overlapping and blending with the next, assisting in welding together the unit we recognize as the human voice. Posture is the foundation, articulation the end product.

Anyone who has read the text of EMERGENT VOICE in its regular order to this point is well aware that posture and respiration caused us to consider phonation, that explanations about phonation led us into resonation, and that to fully explain resonation we were compelled to discuss the basic relationship of fundamental and overtones in the articulation of vowels.

We will approach articulation from three different angles. First, the origin of vowels and consonants from the vegetative actions of sucking, chewing, and swallowing. Second, the muscular activities of their overlapping and blending in speech and singing. Third, their application to voice training through the dynamic phonetics developed by the author's investigations.

For a quarter of a century the writer made careful observations concerning the muscle movements of vowels and consonants in his private pupils. From a thorough study of phonetics and his empirical findings, he wrote the text which he called "Modern Phonetization Applied to Singing."[1] During the same time that he was making his empirical observations, Shohara[2] at the University of Michigan was conducting a thorough scientific investigation into sucking, chewing, and swallowing and their adaptation to speech. Paralleling these two investigations in muscle movements, was a long line of research in the acoustics of vowels by physicists and sound engineers, culminating in the work of Miller[3] in the "Science of Musical Sounds" and Fletcher[4] in "Speech and Hearing." From these three opposite approaches: empirical observation in voice students, a scientific investigation of vegetative functions adapted to speech, and a study of sound wave frequencies in vowel forms, the same order of vowels emerged.

No two individuals pronounce the same vowel alike in muscle actions. All individuals pronounce their vowels by resonant reinforcement of sound waves in the cavities made by modifications of the actions of

---

[1] Westerman, Kenneth N. *Modern Phonetization Applied to Singing.* Ann Arbor, Michigan, Box 62: Modern Phonetization, 1936 (second edition).

[2] Shohara, Hide. *Genesis of the Articulatory Movements of Speech with Special Reference to the Processes of Sucking, Chewing, and Swallowing.* Doctoral dissertation, University of Michigan, 1932.

[3] Miller, D.C. *The Science of Musical Sounds.* New York: Macmillan, 1926.

[4] Fletcher, Harvey D. *Speech and Hearing.* New York: Van Nostrand, 1929.

sucking, chewing, and swallowing. These cavities are formed by muscle movements of the throat, jaw, soft palate, uvula, tongue, and lips, and their reflected action on the hyoid bone and larynx. The actions of the jaw, tongue, soft palate, and uvula are primary. Lip action is secondary. The vowel formant is a result, not a cause.

When the writer made the statement in the paragraph above, that "No two individuals pronounce the same vowel alike in muscle actions" he was not making a snap judgment from empirical observation but a well considered statement of a proven fact after years of careful investigations. All the actions of throat, jaw, tongue, soft palate, uvula, and lips in the formation of the complete vowel series from $\bar{e}$ to $\overline{oo}$ are in relationship to the shape of the arch of the hard and soft palate and teeth formations.

As an initial investigation in this field, the author took seven different measurements (heights, depths, widths) on 130 casts of hard palate arches of different individuals. After the data was compiled, he had an engineer run his slide rule on the results and found that, considering the arch of the hard palate *only*, in the 140,000,000 inhabitants of the United States only two people would articulate alike in muscle actions. If one took into consideration the added variations in soft palates, uvulas, pharyngeal walls, palatine arches, jaws, teeth formations, tongues, cheeks, and lips, no two individuals could possibly pronounce the same vowel alike in muscle actions if they sang the same vowel formant. Plate VI shows the four principle hard palate arch forms. It is thought by Muyskens [5] and the author that there is a definite correlation between arch forms and dominance in the ductless gland setup of individuals. No. III, Plate VI is thought to be a pure pituitary type. The innumerable mixtures of the four types shown in Plate VI make it absolutely necessary for the voice teacher to study carefully the natural articulation of each student, that no muscle strain is developed in jaw or tongue action when singing.

If vowel formants are to be identical acoustically, so that the relationship of fundamental and overtones give identical quality in perception, the muscle actions of all individuals must vary enormously, for vowel formants are produced by muscle movements, and the muscle movements of larynx, pharyngeal walls, soft palate, uvula, jaw, tongue, cheeks, and lips must be made in relationship to the forms of soft and hard palate arches and teeth formations. Just a glance at Illustrations I and III of Plate VI will show anyone the utter futility as well as the terrible muscle strain imposed on some students by forcing them to use the same mouth opening for the same vowel. When the author was making his investigation in the speech of the deaf at the speech clinic

[5] Muyskens, John Henry, Professor of Phonetics and Biolinguistics, University of Michigan.

at the University of Michigan, he was able to make totally deaf individuals speak normally when he took into consideration all the facts bearing on the muscle actions of articulation and their resultant reverberation feels. A precise and accurate study of the articulation habits of each individual in relationship to arch formations combined with his normal habits of chewing and swallowing, can develop in the student of singing a complete and natural emergence of resonation into articulation.

When an individual chews a mouthful of food, he finally rolls it into a ball (bolus) with his tongue, and by a progressive action of lips, cheeks, tongue, soft palate, and throat, passes the bolus back into the esophagus and it is carried down to the stomach. As a rule an individual chews on one side of his mouth and swallows down the other. The side of the mouth on which he chews is generally the last to move when he smiles, for the muscles are so tense from chewing that they do not let go for a smile as quickly as the swallowing side. The cavity down which the food is carried is seldom in the center of the mouth. It almost always lies to right or left of center. Some people are right-handed chewers and left-handed swallowers, some left-handed chewers and right-handed swallowers, while a few are ambidextrous. A few chew and swallow on the same side, depending on deformities of teeth and roofs of mouths, or teeth extractions.

Sound vibrations produced at the vocal lips, passing into the bolus cavity of the progressive swallowing act, form vowels. Starting with the vowel $\bar{e}$ as in *veal* (small, tense, very far forward in the mouth, in fact a tube only about half the diameter of a lead pencil between the tongue and the roof of the mouth), as the cavity progresses backward, through the swallowing act, the last few vowels are synchronized with a sucking action by the lips, ending with vowel $\overline{oo}$ as in *room,* in which (contrary to current belief) the lip action is secondary. The order of vowels, taken back through the synchronized swallowing and sucking act in their alternating tense and lax positions are $\bar{e}$ *(veal)*, $\breve{i}$ *(sing)*; $\bar{a}$ *(take)*, $\breve{e}$ *(them)*; $\breve{a}$ *(shall)*, $\ddot{a}$ *(large)*; $\breve{o}$ *(got)*, $\breve{u}$ *(dust)*; $\hat{o}$ *(gorgeous)*, $\breve{u}$ *(dust)*; $\bar{o}$ *(note)*, $\hat{u}$ *(pull)*; $\overline{oo}$ *(room)*, $\breve{oo}$ *(book)*. Whether examined empirically by watching voice students, scientifically by swallowing and sucking actions, or acoustically for numbers of vibrations per second—the above order emerges.

Divided into swallowing and sucking groups they can be listed $\bar{e}$, $\breve{i}$, $\bar{a}$, $\breve{e}$, $\breve{a}$, $\ddot{a}$, as a *swallowing progression,* and $\breve{o}$, $\hat{o}$, $\breve{u}$, $\bar{o}$, $\hat{u}$, $\overline{oo}$ as a *sucking progression.*

For the individual to become acquainted with the vowel forms in himself, the student should pronounce the vowels of the swallowing group before a mirror and watch and feel the progression of the tongue, jaw, and lip action in $\bar{e}$, $\breve{i}$, $\bar{a}$, $\breve{e}$, $\breve{a}$, $\ddot{a}$. He should then repeat the process, using the sucking group, *ŏ, ô, ŭ, ọ, û, ōō*. He should then join the groups together using the lax form *ä* as in *large* as the center and pronounce *ē, ǐ, ā, ĕ, ă, ä, ô, ŭ, ō, û, ōō*, three times through, watching tongue and larynx the first time, jaw the second time, and lips the third time. This will let him become acquainted with the blending of the swallowing and sucking acts in *his own* natural vowel forms. These vowel forms are not the same in any two individuals. They not only vary between individuals, but vary in speech in the same individual through the overlapping and blending of the muscle actions of the preceding and succeeding consonants and vowels.

The tense forms of *ē, ā, ă, ŏ, ô, ō, ōō* show the complete swallowing and sucking progression most distinctly, while the lax forms of *ǐ, ĕ, ä, ŭ*, and *ōō* are not so definite in perception. However, these lax forms are of utmost importance in the English language for they account for about one-third of all the sounds on the written page, including both consonants and vowels. Our language is constantly dropping tense forms in favor of the more quickly pronounced lax forms. This is caused mostly by the overlapping and blending of the articulation of consonants with vowel forms.

The true concept of what actually constitutes the basis of articulation was never known until the remarkable work done by Muyskens [6] at the University of Michigan on the "Hypha," the physiological syllable caused by the opening and closing of the vocal tract. The concept of Muyskens gives us a true and specific judgment for both speech and singing and for the first time makes us aware of the co-ordination in the openings and closures at the lips, tongue, nasal port, and vocal lips and defines the outlines of a physiological syllable. Through this concept we are able to make judgments of the energy surges used in articulation and their location so that the overlapping and blending of words in singing may be clean and clear while still maintaining that smooth, legato flow so essential to true artistry.

Vowel forms have no meanings. Only as they are put into the framework of consonantal closures do they come to life. At least it would be rather difficult to communicate our ideas with only "ah" and "oh," the two exclamations arising from vowel forms. Closures of the vocal tract (consonants) are the dynamic outlines of words, and as such, need to be as thoroughly understood as vowels, if the singer is to communicate his thoughts, emotions, passions, and moods to his audience.

Consonants are in groups, similarly produced as far as the position of the tongue, lips, and jaw are concerned, but varied by being *breathy, voiced,* or *hummed*. (This is a general statement and should be ac-

6 Muyskens, John Henry. *The Hypha*. Doctoral dissertation, University of Michigan, 1925.

cepted only in the light of succeeding statements concerning overlapping and blending.)

Three of the groups have all three forms:

The 1st group is formed by closing the lips: *p* as in *push,* *b* as in *bounce,* *m* as in *might;* *p* being breathy, *b* voiced, and *m* hummed.

The 2nd group is formed by the tip of the tongue rising to the gums in back of the upper teeth and snapping down: *t* as in *take,* *d* as in *dust,* and *n* as in *note;* *t* being breathy, *d* being voiced and *n* being hummed.

The 3rd group is formed by the tongue being raised against the palate: hard *c* (*k*) as in *call,* *g* as in *gone,* *ng* as in *song;* *c* (*k*) breathy, *g* being voiced, *ng* being hummed.

There are five groups which have only breath and voice forms *without the humming form* because it is impossible to hum in the position required for pronouncing them. They are:

1st. The puckered lip group: *wh* as in *where,* *w* as in *were;* *wh* being breathy, *w* being voiced.

2nd. The lower lip brushed lightly against the upper teeth: *f* as in *feet,* *v* as in *veal;* *f* being *breathy,* *v* being voiced.

3rd. The tongue between the teeth: *th* as in *thin,* *th'* as in *then;* *th* breathy, *th'* voiced.

4th. This group is formed by starting to close the jaw from the position of a short *ĭ* and hissing the breath through the small opening on the tip of the tongue: *s* as in *sing,* *z* as in *zero;* *s* being breathy, *z* being voiced.

5th. The last group having breath and voice forms is the one formed by starting to close the jaw from the position of tense *ă* and hissing the breath through the opening on the tip of the tongue and through the teeth: *sh* as in *shall,* *zh* as in *pleasure;* *sh* being breathy, *zh* being voiced.

There is one voiced pair that is used for both consonants and vowels; the *l* as in *large* and *trouble* and the *r* as in *room* and *mother.* In this pair the tip of the tongue is raised to the gums in back of the upper teeth and snapped or curled down with a flip of the tip. (This is a general description of the French or Italian *r* used in singing and not of the American *r* which is a form of pulling back and bunching the tip tongue muscles.)

There is one form of pure breath: *h* as in *has,* produced by partially opening the throat and making a quick stroke with the abdominal lift.

The one form of pure voice: *y* as in *yet,* is produced by pronouncing long *ē* and breaking it open with a downward stroke of the jaw.

The final group is made up of combinations. There are four in this group: *x* which is really *ks* as in *ax* or *gz* as in *exact*, *q* which is really *k-hw* as in *quiet*, *ch* which is really a blended *t-sh* as in *chair*, and *j* which is really a blended *d-zh* as in *judge*.

The three groups having all three forms must be thoroughly understood, for they represent the use of the four valves involved in the pronunciation of all vowels and consonants, the *lips*, the *tongue*, the *nasal port*, and the *vocal lips*. All problems in articulation result from the use of these four valves. They are constantly in motion during speech or singing: the lips opening and closing; the tongue shaping vowels or closing against the roof of the mouth or the teeth; the nasal port (the doorway to the nose opened and closed by the muscles of the soft palate, uvula, and pharynx) opening or closing for consonants or vowels; and the vocal lips opening for breathing and breathy consonants or closing for tones and voiced consonants.

The **Lip Group**, *p, b, m*, if pronounced as letters, sound *pee, bee, em*, but when said as consonants, are muscle actions resulting in sounds as in the words, *push, bounce, might*.

To find the formation of *p*, pronounce *push* lightly. The lips and nasal port are closed. The valve of the tongue and the vocal lips are open. We find that it is pronounced by breath only, exploded through the closed lips.

The formation of *b* is identical with *p* in lip, tongue, and nasal port position, but the vocal lips are closed and the voice is used. Pronounce *bounce* and one will discover that *b* is not pronounced by exploded breath but by voice in the mouth cavity only, released by parting the lips. Hold the *b* as long as possible and one will find the mouth will get so full of breath from the tone vibrations that the sound will cease if the lips are not parted. Close the nose while pronouncing *b* and one will find that the nasal passages are already blocked by a closed nasal port and not necessary to its pronunciation.

The *m* is identical with *p* and *b* as far as lip and tongue are concerned, but the nasal port is now open and the tone, voiced like the *b*, is hummed through the nose. The *m* consonant plays a very vital part in voice culture because of its perfect lip, tongue, and jaw co-ordination and its use of the passages above the roof of the mouth. One cannot overestimate its worth in early vocalizing for it trains the opening of the nasal port while jaw, lips, and tongue are in lax condition ready for pronunciation. Its significance to the student of voice in comparison with *n* and *ng* is thoroughly analyzed and discussed in the chapter on *Humming*.

The **Tip-Tongue Group**, *t, d*, and *n*, if pronounced as letters, sound *tee, dee* and *en*, but when used as consonants have the sounds as in the words, *take, dust*, and *note*.

To find the formation of *t*, pronounce the word *take* and one will find that the tip of the tongue rises and is snapped down releasing the breath held in the mouth. It corresponds exactly with *p* of the lip group except that the tip of the tongue forms the closure instead of the lips.

The formation of *d* is practically the same as *t* in tongue position but very little breath is used, the *d* being voiced. Pronounce *dust* and one will discover that *d* is not pronounced by exploded breath but by tone vibrations held in the mouth behind the tongue and released when the tongue is snapped down from its position against the roof of the mouth. By pinching the nostrils one will also discover that in the pronunciation of *d*, the nasal port is closed.

The *n* is identical with *t* and *d* in tongue position but the nasal port is open and the voiced breath, instead of being held in the mouth as in *d*, flows freely through the nasal passages as in *m*. Pronounce the word *note*, holding the *n*, and one will be impressed with the fine clearness of the light hum resulting from the *n* consonant. It holds a place second only to *m* in assisting the training of the use of the nasal passages. It also is more thoroughly discussed in the chapter on *Humming*.

The **Tongue-Against-the-Palate Group**, *k*, *g*, and *ng*, if pronounced as letters, would be *kay*, *gee*, and *engee*, but when used as consonants have the sound as in the words, *call*, *gone*, and *song*.

To find the formation of *k* or hard *c*, pronounce the word *call* and one will notice that the closure of the tongue valve has now moved back on the palate. With the pronunciation of *p*, the lips formed the closure; with *t*, the tip of the tongue; but in *call*, the body of the tongue rises against the palate making the closure, and the *k* is pronounced by the breath escaping as the tongue is released. In the pronunciation of *k* the lip valve is open, the tongue valve closed, the nasal port closed, and the vocal lips open.

The formation of *g* is identical with *k* except that the voiced tone is blocked by the tongue and the nasal port, and released by dropping the tongue from its position against the palate. By pronouncing the words *bounce*, *dust*, and *gone*, it will be seen that *b*, *d*, and *g* are all voiced consonants blocked successively by lips, tip of tongue, and tongue against the palate, and that all three use the closed nasal port, leaving all vibrations in the mouth. With the exception of *m, n, ng,* and sometimes *l* and *r*, all voiced and breathy consonants synchronize the closing of the nasal port with the closure at the lips or tongue.

The formation of *ng* is similar in tongue position with *k* and *g*, although generally farther back in the mouth. Pronounce the word *song* and again as in *m* and *n* the nasal port opens, the nasal passages become free, and the *ng* is hummed through the nose. *Ng*, unlike *m* and *n* has a decided tendency toward making the vowel which precedes it, sound with a nasal twang. This is caused by the back of the tongue pushing against the soft palate and partially closing the nasal port. We have already reported in the chapter on *Resonation* that a nasal twang is only caused by partial closure of the nasal passages. Even some of our best artists sing with a very decided twang on words like *long, sing,* and *song.* Only with voices that have a decidedly flat, harsh, and raspy quality should the *ng* ever be used in vocalizing exercises.

OVERLAPPING AND BLENDING

The muscle movements involved in the overlapping and blending of consonants and vowels in speech and singing can only be understood by consciously becoming aware again, as in early childhood, through sight, muscle action, kinesthetic sense (muscle sense), and touch and pressure, of the movements of lips, tongue, soft palate, jaw and throat in articulation. The following chart, a modification of one developed by the author for teaching normal speech to the deaf, will give to the student a thorough insight into articulation tendencies.

For the chart to have any worth to the student, no letters must be pronounced as letters, but *must* be pronounced as *muscle actions* in words. For example, in the preceding sentence, *m* is never *em* but in *must* and *muscle* is actually a humming sound produced by closed lips, open tongue valve, an open nasal port, and closed vocal lips. The muscle actions of the closed lips, the lax tongue, the open nasal port synchronized with the voice produced at the vocal lips constitute its pronunciation—it is never the letter *em* when used in a word.

The use of *O-e, oa, -o, ow,* in the chart, is to show the many spellings of the pure *O* vowel form. This will assist the individual in recognizing the *spelling* used for the different vowels. Without this help, the chart would be useless to deaf students. Most of us have never noticed that *a* is almost never *A* except in words closing in *e* as *take, late, hate, lake,* and that exceptions as in *have* are so few that they are simple in explanation to the totally deaf.

Take the letter *e* at the bottom of the vowel chart. As pronounced in *veal* it has its letter sound; but in the lax form of *ā* it becomes *ĕ* as in *them.* Its own lax form is *ĭ* as in *sit* or in *English* and when only partially lax it becomes a cross between *ē* (as in *veal*) and *ĭ* (as in *sit*) as in e*vent* or e*vaporate.* When thoroughly lax it passes on, even further yet, to a pure *ŭ* as in *dust.* In rapid conversation as in the second syllable of such words as *recent* and *covenant* it has this completely lax form of *ŭ.*

To thoroughly understand the significance of the Consonant and Vowel Chart and its application to speech and singing, one would need

AN EMERGENT CHART
OF
CONSONANTS AND VOWELS
FOR STUDYING OVERLAPPING AND BLENDING OF MUSCLE ACTIONS

CONSONANTS

Hummed	Voiced	Breath
		H (home)
M (might)	B (bounce)	P (pull)
	W (were)	WH (hw)(where)
	V (veal)	F (ph)(feel)(phone)
N (note)	D (dust)	T (take)
	TH(them)	TH (thin)
	L (large)	L (flip)(under speed)
	R (er,ur,ir,ar,or,re)	R (trip)(under speed)
	Z (s)(zebra)(these)	S (sit)(c-e)(c-i)(c-y)
	J (job)(g)(dge)	CH (tch)(chum)
	ZH (s)(pleasure)	SH (shall)
	Y	
NG (song)	G (gone)	K (c)(ck)(call)(kick)

Combinations
qu (khw)(quiet)
x (ks)(tax)

* * *

VOWELS

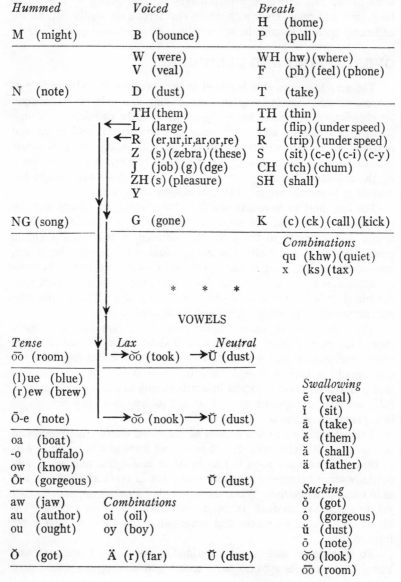

Tense	Lax	Neutral
ōō (room)	ŏŏ (took)	Ŭ (dust)
(l)ue (blue)		
(r)ew (brew)		
Ō-e (note)	ŏŏ (nook)	Ŭ (dust)
oa (boat)		
-o (buffalo)		
ow (know)		
Ôr (gorgeous)		Ŭ (dust)
aw (jaw)	*Combinations*	
au (author)	oi (oil)	
ou (ought)	oy (boy)	
Ŏ (got)	Ä (r)(far)	Ŭ (dust)

Swallowing
ē (veal)
ĭ (sit)
ā (take)
ĕ (them)
ă (shall)
ä (father)

Sucking
ŏ (got)
ô (gorgeous)
ŭ (dust)
ō (note)
ŏŏ (look)
ōō (room)

Ă (has)	Ä (father)	Ŭ (dust)	*Combinations*
			ou (bounce)
			ow (now)
Ā-e (take)	Ĕ (them)	Ŭ (dust)	
ai (bait)			i-e (kite)
			igh (might)
Ēa (veal)	Ĭ (sit)	Ŭ (dust)	-y (why)
ee (feel)	*Combinations*		
e-e (mete)	u- (use)		
	u-e (cute)		
	ew (few)		

to start with the hummed *m* consonant, and progressing through the voiced *b* to the breathy *p*, check the muscle actions: *m*—closed lips, lax tongue, voiced, open nasal port; *b*—closed lips, lax tongue, voiced, closed nasal port; *p*—closed lips, lax tongue, voiceless (open vocal lips), closed nasal port; but all pronounced by closing and parting the lips. To the casual observer they all look alike, but to the clever speech reader (lip reader) the *m* is long and freely held, the *b* is medium and tensely held, the *p* very short and explosive. Progressing on down through the entire chart, every consonant and vowel should be checked for muscle action, from left to right (on the chart).

One acquires enormous respect for the intensive work done by a child between the ages of six months and three years when he develops all these actions, and patterns and conditions them into automatic use.

One is surprised to discover that *l* and *r* when used as vowels, as in *trouble* and *were*, have perfect co-ordination with the o͝o vowel as in *look*, thus answering the question: "What vowel should be sung in words like 'wo*r*ld,' 'he*r*,' 'we*r*e,' 'mothe*r*,' 'troub*l*e,' etc.?" *R* and *l* should never be sung as vowels but should be given the quick, clean enunciation of consonants, the o͝o vowel being sung as the vowel form in their stead.

It will be noticed, by studying the chart, that all vowels become *ŭ* (the neutral vowel) in their final lax position. Anyone can easily check this shifting muscle action by pronouncing the vowels of the chart from left to right in Tense, Lax, Neutral order. For example, take the vowel o͞o as in *room*, at the beginning of the Vowel Chart. Because the vowel o͞o originally emerged from the tense sucking position of the lips, the o͞o form still has tendencies in most words toward lip puckering. (The lip puckering, however, is not primary, for $\overline{oo}$ can be pronounced perfectly with no lip action. With a mirror, pronounce the word *loose* while smiling.)

If, after vigorously pronouncing, by itself, the $\overline{oo}$ as in *room*, one allows lips and tongue to become lax without moving the jaw, the $\overline{oo}$ changes to $\breve{oo}$ as in *look*. If one increases the size of the cavity between tongue and roof of mouth by a slightly more lax jaw position, the $\overline{oo}$ becomes further modified to $\breve{u}$ as in *dust*, the neutral vowel form. In the English language, the change from the tense $\overline{oo}$ form to the lax form of $\breve{oo}$ has become nearly universal. In words ending with k, the change has become complete, as in *look, book, shook, took,* etc. Where the preceding and succeeding consonants are both well forward in the mouth, the tense $\overline{oo}$ form still remains, as in *moon, room, boon, soon,* etc. Several very interesting forms are now in the process of changing, as in *roof* and *hoof.* Because of the f consonant at the close, it is slightly difficult to maintain the natural sucking position of the lips for the tense $\overline{oo}$, so the forms $r\breve{oo}f$ and $h\breve{oo}f$ are often heard in conversation instead of the so-called correct forms, $r\overline{oo}f$ and $h\overline{oo}f$. The last Edition of Webster's New International Dictionary states: "cultivated usage is divided between $\overline{oo}$ and $\breve{oo}$ in *hoof, roof, hoop, root, soot, whooping cough . . .*"

Let us take the word *roof* for example. The architect who has just completed the new theatre next to the author's studio in Ann Arbor calls the $r\overline{oo}f$ a $r\breve{oo}f$. He knows that $r\overline{oo}f$ is the dictionary pronunciation, but the speed of muscle action in ordinary conversation has already changed the tense $\overline{oo}$ to the lax $\breve{oo}$ form in the conversation of his laborers. His real reason for pronouncing it $r\breve{oo}f$ is that he wishes his laborers to think him friendly and not "high-hat." Out of courtesy to the architect, the architect's friends begin to call it a $r\breve{oo}f$ for they do not wish to embarrass him by correcting his pronunciation. In a few more dictionaries the percentage of use of $r\breve{oo}f$ will exceed 50 per cent and the editors will place $r\breve{oo}f$ as the proper pronunciation in the dictionary. The author knows that such changes are inevitable, for *usage controls English pronunciation, and easy muscle actions control usage.* That does not mean that the author has his students sing $r\breve{oo}f$ for $r\overline{oo}f$. He doesn't. He will wait until the dictionary recognizes the change.

One of the places where speed of muscle action in pronunciation is making great changes in English speech, is in the overlapping of consonants in the $\bar{u}$ vowel as in *few*. The 1953 Webster's[7] says: "after r, the y element is now completely silent in standard speech as in *rule* (rool), *brew* (broo), *true* (troo), etc. In *assume* . . . . cultivated speakers in both England and America often suppress the first element of the

---

[7] Webster's Collegiate Dictionary. Springfield, Mass.: G. & C. Merriam Co., 1953 (sixth edition).

ū, leaving *ōō*. After *d* (duty), *t* (tune), *n* (new) . . . in America, at least, the *ōō* sound is widely used by the educated. . . ." This change has now become so complete in educated circles in America, that on most university campuses the only "steeoodents" are in the Speech and English Departments—all the rest are "stoodents."

If we drop back only as far as the 1914 Edition of Webster's New International, we will find the dictionary builders rather bothered by this inevitable change which was starting even then to shift the so-called *y* element in *ū* to an *ĭ* and seemed to be progressing toward full adoption of the pure *ōō* sound. We find this warning: "It is not . . . . proper to omit the initial element entirely, and thus reduce the *ū* to simple *ōō*." If we compare that attitude with the quotations cited above from the 1953 Edition, we notice one of the fundamental laws of the English language—*usage controls our language*—it is never static as some teachers of speech and English would have our youth believe. Just as our life has progressed from oxcart days to airplanes and automobiles, so our speech is speeding up, moving forward in the mouth, and taking short-cuts because of speed in the overlapping and blending of muscle actions.

The author knows that the following statement will create antagonism in the minds of all who cling to the past, but it is his firm belief that *it is better to err on the side of inevitable progress than to try to cling to antiquated forms which are passing out of ordinary cultured conversational use.*

The author knows that many of his readers will have studied with voice teachers who have felt it their "deeyooty" to see that they allowed no "neeyoo" pronunciations to creep into their "steeyoodents' teeyoons." (All according to the dictionary but with the *e* element enormously overdone.) If one listens to a full evening concert of an artist who uses such exaggerated pronunciations, he will feel like the two people the author overheard leaving such a concert, "What a glorious voice, but what makes his articulation sound so odd?" and the reply, "I couldn't tell you what it is, but it sounds stilted and overdone to me." It would make no difference how glorious the voice, how charming the personality, how exceptional the interpretative ability, any singer who is not taught the normal overlapping and blending of cultured conversational English can be doomed to third rate mediocrity when he might stand at the top of his profession. It does not pay either in artistry or popularity to cling too tenaciously to old forms of pronunciation.

We said at the beginning of this chapter that artistic singing demanded pure vowel forms and quickly pronounced, clean and clear consonants. After the above discussion, some readers will be asking, "If one is to sing pure vowel forms and they are constantly changing, how will the singer know what to use?" The student, the teacher of voice, and the choral conductor should be the best trained and the most "up-to-the-minute" individuals in the educational world in knowledge of present usage and trends of pronunciation in spoken English. They should know how the word in question arrived at its *present* pronunciation. Take the second syllable of the word *present* above. In rapid conversation it is merely *nt*, leaving the *e* out, the *n* consonant being used as a vowel between the *z* (s) and *t*. If sung in its original form, *ĕ* (as in *sent*), it sounds overdone. Sung in its conversational form *nt*, it becomes ridiculous. If one will look at its emergence in the Vowel Chart (on page 52) he sees the *ā* Tense, *ĕ* Lax, *ŭ* Neutral progression. If sung with a vowel color about half-way between *ĕ* and *ŭ* with the *nt* blended together as a final consonant, it becomes normal to the listener's ear. Judgments of this type are constantly before the soloist, teacher, and choral conductor and some of the most humorous things heard before the public, are caused by lack of knowledge of the origin and trends of the word in question: "Deep Riv*ah*" (riv*er*), "W*air* (w*ere*) you there," (both should be *ōō*); "Oh the pretty, pretty crea-*tēēōōr*" (should be *chōōr*). The sign *tū* in the dictionary in words like *nature, future, literature,* etc., actually means *chōōr* but most people do not take the time to study the 275 paragraphs on pronunciation at the beginning of the dictionary to find what the signs mean, so they sing and speak fancy, complicated things of their own invention instead of the simple, natural pronunciations of normal conversation. The 1953 Edition of Webster's Collegiate Dictionary says: "In words like *nature, verdure,* the off-glide of the *t* or *d* combines with the first element of *u*" to make different forms, but "*ch* or *j* . . . . is the natural pronunciation in general use by *unaffected* speakers in all common words."

Any pronunciation other than that used in cultured conversation appears to be an affectation when sung. "Affectation" is "an attempt to assume or exhibit what is not natural or real; false display; artificial show." The vocal student needs careful training in normal, cultured pronunciation if he ever expects to deliver a real message from the thoughts, emotions, passions, and moods of his poems, for the slightest deviation gives to the public the impression of insincerity. *The latest edition of a standard dictionary is always the true source of information.* Even the dictionary may be wrong, for it may be years behind the times in having certain changes reported. In conversation the final syllable of the word *attention* has been *chn* for many years, but even the 1953 dictionaries still record it as *shŭn,* which is only used for commands in the army. The word *forest* is still recorded as *fŏr'ĕst* in spite of a general American usage of *fôr'ĭst* with the pronunciation of the first syllable approximating that of the conjunction *for,* and the second, a cross between an *ĕ* and an *ĭ*, caused by the *st* closure. If a soloist should sing "I heard a *fŏr′ ĕst* praying," [8] with the prolongation of the vowels necessary for the accuracy of production, using the *ŏ* and *ĕ* vowels in their pure form as the dictionary states, his audience would find its whole attention focused on his pronunciation rather than on the prayer.

To further emphasize the fact that we are dealing with muscle actions, and not with letters or even sounds (except as muscle actions produce those sounds), let us notice briefly the influence of consonants on vowels and vowels on consonants. Careful observation with a mirror, giving close attention to touch and pressure sense, while pronouncing the words *team* and *keep*, will show that the influence of the *t* and *k* changes the position of the *ē* formation. Repeat, using the words *beak* and *book*, and one will discover that the *ē* and *o͞o* have influenced the pronunciation of the *k* as to its point of contact with the roof of the mouth. A knowledge of these tendencies is of great importance to the choral conductor and voice teacher who wish pure artistry in public performance, for many times these influences have shaded the vowel slightly toward a more tense or lax form, and the form which eyesight in spelling would choose for singing purposes, would create in the mind of an audience a feeling that the soloist or choir was not normal in pronunciation.

Nearly all voice teachers have confined their vocalizing to the five Italian vowels *i, e, a, o, u,* (*ē, ā, ä, ō, o͞o*). These account for a meager 12 per cent of the sounds on the written page in English while the English syllable *si* as in *sit* accounts for over 12 per cent. The lax vowels *ĭ, ĕ, ä, ŭ, o͝o* (*û*) and the tense *ă*, and the consonantal muscular activities account for the other 88 per cent in English.

Vowels do not make words. Vowels may be all mispronounced and words still understood, if consonants are distinctly articulated. Pure artistry, however, lies in absolute purity of vowel articulation with consonantal actions overlapped and blended with such speed that they never interfere with the resonant flow of the changing vowels.

The overlapping and blending of consonants between vowels presents a distinct problem for the voice teacher and choral conductor which is so sadly neglected by some that the work of their soloists and choral groups becomes distressingly funny at times. Every soloist and ensemble is merely a mirror of the teacher's knowledge of his profession. This is as it should be, for it gives a discerning adjudicator the opportunity to even recognize the source of the conductor's musical education through his students' work and to lay the blame for imperfect production, not on Susie Jones from Podunk Center, but back on Prof. X

---

[8] Song by Peter De Rose, *"I Heard a Forest Praying."* New York: Chappell & Co., Inc., 1937.

at the State Normal who taught Susie's teacher that the proper vowel to sing in *er* is *ä* (which it isn't), and that the consonantal ending of one word should always be separated from the consonantal beginning of the next (which it shouldn't), who thinks that the musical phrase is more important than the thought phrase in vocal music (which it isn't), and who allows students to sing in public before even the most basic controls for voice production have become automatic.

The rule for the blending of consonants between words in singing is very simple. It is exactly the same as in speech except that great care is necessary, in singing, *that the* **energy surge** *be at the beginning of words and not on the close of the preceding word.* For example in "Drink to me only with thine eyes and I will pledge with mine": in "with thine" the two *th*'s blend together forming a long *th,* but an **energy surge** on the *th* of "thine" leaves no doubt of the word. If the energy surges are right, "thine eyes and I will" will sound normal. If not, they would sound like "thy neye zan die will." Lack of knowledge of the above simple law of overlapping and blending in articulation creates choppy singing through separation of words that do not need to be separated. Many voice teachers and choral conductors when seeing a phrase like "who has died for us" think it absolutely necessary to make the phrase sound choppy, by separating "hast" from "died" and "died" from "for," and singing "hast-ŭ-died-ŭ-for." It is no more difficult in singing, for the tongue to go up a *t* and come down a *d* in "hast died" than it is in speech, or to go up a *d* and blend into the *f* lip action in "died for."

It is one of the author's favorite illustrations to say to a class on "articulation overlapping and blending," that until they can describe the pronunciation of the three *k*'s in "The old *c*ow hoo*k*ed the *c*at," they are not prepared to understand articulation problems as they arise in choral and solo singing. The first *k* is pronounced by a downward stroke of the tongue only, the second *k* by an upward stroke only, the third *k* by an upward and downward stroke, the overlapping of the *d,* the *t-th,* and the *ŭ* and *ä* vowels causing the three forms.

An odd overlapping was brought recently to the author's attention by a voice student. The overlap of the words "has seen" had been marked as separate words and the student warned to be sure that he separated the two *s*'s. When the author said, "There aren't two *s*'s," the student said, "Sure there are—the one on the end of 'has' and the one on the beginning of 'seen'." The author explained that "has" ends in a *z,* not an *s* and that the *z* is voiced while the initial *s* of "seen" is breathy and that the overlapping and blending of the two can be sung the same as when spoken, by merely putting an energy surge on the initial *s* of "seen" when the breathy *s* starts the word. There is no necessity for separating such words.

DYNAMIC PHONETICS

We have thoroughly discussed the origin of vowels and consonants from the life maintaining activities of the body and have explained the muscular actions of their overlapping and blending. We are now ready to study their application to voice training through the dynamic phonetics developed by the author's investigations.

The muscular actions of certain consonants assist in vowel formations. By combining these into syllables it is possible for the voice student to develop speed and accuracy in articulation allowing full and free resonation to feed that articulation. This is necessary to make the modifications of speech into singing and have enunciation both accurate and artistic.

After many years of careful investigation of muscle movements in articulation, the author evolved a series of dynamic phonetic syllables for application to articulation problems which have proved to be of inestimable worth in voice training. They are English syllables from English words. Instead of the meager 12 per cent which the Italian vowels represent, they cover over 90 per cent of the sounds on the written page and over 95 per cent of the muscle movements. Used as the basis for vocal practice in the emergence from resonation into articulation, they assist in the development of enormous ranges and freedom of production in a minimum of time. Because the consonantal muscle action assists the vowel formation, they can be pronounced at the rate of 10 to a second. Their ease of pronunciation makes them practically foolproof in articulation exercises. Used following an *m*-hum, they develop a true concept of uniformity in resonation impossible by any other method of approach.

Arranged in vowel order, they are:

vē   as in *ve*al
sĭ   as in *si*t
tā   as in *ta*ke
thĕ as in *the*m
shă as in *sha*ll
lä   as in *la*rge
gô   as in *go*ne   (midwestern pronun-
                     ciation as *gaw*n)
dŭ   as in *du*st
nō   as in *no*te
pû   as in *pu*sh
rōō as in *roo*m
mī   as in *mi*ght
bou as in *bou*nce
few as in *few*
coi as in *coi*n

Arranged in consonantal order, they are:

LIP	TIP-TONGUE
mī as in *might*	nō as in *note*
bou as in *bou*nce	dŭ as in *du*st
pû as in *pu*sh	tā as in *take*
vē as in *veal*	rōō as in *roo*m
few as in *few*	lä as in *large*
	thĕ as in *the*m
TONGUE AGAINST PALATE	sĭ as in *sit*
gô as in *gone* (midwestern *gaw*n)	shă as in *sha*ll
coi as in *coi*n	

Arranged for vocalizing purposes using contrasting muscle actions for greater facility in articulation, and with definite problems of resonation in each group, they are:

I.	II.
la as in *large*	*la* as in *large*
mi as in *might*	*the* as in *the*m
no as in *note*	*ta* as in *take*
go as in *gone*	*du* as in *du*st

III.	IV.
la as in *large*	*pu* as in *pu*sh
sha as in *sha*ll	*go* as in *gone*
bou as in *bou*nce	*ve* as in *veal*
si as in *sit*	*roo* as in *roo*m

In the arrangement above, for vocalizing purposes, certain changes have been made. The combinations (diphthongs) *oi* and *ū* as in *coin* and *few* (*u*nite) are left out. The two combined, only account for four-tenths of 1 per cent of the sounds on the written page and the elements used in making them are included in other syllables; even the $c(k)$ and *f* are merely the voiceless forms of *g* and *v* which appear in *gô* and *ve*. In contrast to the almost insignificant use of *ū* and *oi*, the sounds in the two syllables *du* (*dust*) and *si* (*sit*), neither of which have ever been used for vocalizing purposes, account for over 21 per cent of the sounds on the written page as compared to the meager 12 per cent of the entire Italian vowel series of *i, e, a, o, u*.

The use of the Italian vowels for vocalizing with English students, has resulted in the necessity for an enormous amount of "application work" on songs. This has retarded artistic development in English speaking students. The intelligent use of the above English syllables in vocalizing exercises, cuts the time of application work to a minimum. Through their use, the difference in time for the development of a fully resonant tone, flowing through all words and combinations, can be cut to only a few months for a large percentage of students instead of three to six years as was true under old procedures.

The simplicity of the technique is inseparable with the student's and teacher's knowledge of the muscle movements involved in its use. An *m*-hum followed by singing each group of syllables on a single pitch, concentrating on the full resonation set up in the bony structure of the head by the *m*-hum muscle pattern, will soon develop a perfectly resonant tone through all articulation combinations.

Let us make a short analysis of each group of syllables that we may better understand their use.

Through all vocalizing, the student must always remember the principle discussed in the chapter on *Resonation*: resonation of the pitch tone in the pharynx and above the roof of the mouth is primary and the vowel form secondary as far as beauty of tone quality is concerned.

Group I

lä   as in *la*rge
mī   as in *mi*ght
nō   as in *no*te
gô   as in *go*ne   (midwestern *gaw*n)

In the first group, the consonants present no problem. They are all voiced and the *m* and *n* use an open nasal port. If on a pitch in the middle of the range, one hums with an *m*-hum and follows it with the syllables—as *m*- *lä, mī, nō, gô*—he will find a tendency for the resonation of the *m*-hum to continue through the group. [See Ex. 5, Series II, page 76.] If *lä, mī, nō, gô* is pronounced with a freely moving jaw, the *ī* diphthong in *mī* is sung as an *ä* vowel with the *ĭ* as a vanish just preceding the *nō* and the *g* of the *gô* is released quickly, the whole group will flow along as a resonant unit. The voiced consonants with the nasalized *m* and *n*, make this group the easiest for most students.

Group II

lä   as in *la*rge
thĕ   as in *the*m
tā   as in *ta*ke
dŭ   as in *du*st

In the second group we find two new problems. The vowel forms change in size and the breathy *t* consonant (opening the vocal lips and closing the nasal port) has a tendency to destroy nasalization. Whenever tone vibrations are fully resonated, the articulation of consonants and vowels does not change that resonation, but old habits of nasal port closures are so strong that, with consonants using breath for their pronunciation, as *p, f, th, t, s, sh, ch,* and *k,* which have always been synchronized with the closure of the nasal port, there are tendencies to shift the tone vibrations both to breathy production and increased oralization.

As in the first group, the second group starts with *lä*. This syllable is used as the initial syllable of the first three groups because its perfect correlation of consonant articulation to vowel form and its large size in mouth and jaw action, make it (with *mä*) the ideal vocalizing syllable. The author thinks of this group as the *lax-tense-lax* series. After the lax *lä*, the *thĕ* moves forward in the mouth with a lax, easy muscle feel which becomes more tense in the syllable *tā*, only to become completely lax again with the articulation of *dŭ*. The consonants are all voiced except the *t* and when the legato resonation of the vowels is carried through, there is no resonation problem except care that the *t* does not destroy the full resonation of the succeeding *ā* vowel.

A warning must be given in this group, not to stretch the *dŭ* to a *dä* form. The forms of *ä* as in *lock*, *ŭ* as in *luck*, and *ŏŏ* as in *look*, are merely different distances between the tongue and the roof of the mouth, but they are all lax vowels with no tongue shaping, capable of being pronounced with jaw action only. Because of its intermediate size, the *ŭ* vowel as in *dust*, is called the *neutral vowel* but the *ŏŏ* in its lax position from *ōō* is also without shaping of any kind except that the jaw is more closed than on *ŭ*, while the *ä* vowel is merely a larger position of the *ŭ* form, made by more vigorous jaw action. If the student will say *look, luck, lock* (*ä*), and will study these forms in his own pronunciation he will find the natural positions which make these vowels pure for him. It would be pleasurable to the listening public to hear "Come unto me" instead of the overstretched "Cälm ŏnto mĭ" so often imposed on Sunday morning congregations.

Group III

lä   as in *la*rge
shă   as in *sha*ll
bou   as in *bou*nce
sĭ   as in *si*t

In the third group, *lä, shă, bou, sĭ*, with the breathy *sh* and *s*, it is more difficult to maintain full resonation in the balance of fundamental tone and vowel vibrations. Many voice teachers teach *ä* for *ă*, for singing purposes, because the tenseness of the *ă* formation has a tendency toward oralization of the tone vibrations and a consequent harshness or whiteness of tone quality. In the *lä, shă, bou, sĭ* group, this tendency is emphasized by the breathy *sh* preceding the *ă* vowel. However, its position between the *lä* and *bou* makes it possible, with a little concentration, to have no break in the fullness of resonance through the first three syllables while still maintaining a pure *ă* quality to the vowel. The practice of teaching *ä* for *ă* for singing purposes is one of the greatest sources of affectation in pronunciation by singers. Every vowel should be sung with its true quality if singing articulation is to sound natural to the listening public. The vowel ă accounts for over 4 per cent of the sounds on the written page. When mispronounced, one would hear a false inflection on an average of once in every 25 sounds or once in every 7 vowels. The mispronunciation of ă alone would leave "än impression of äffectation thät would be ät least äbnormal."

Recently the author recorded for his own amusement the ä and ă as sung by a voice teacher who claims that he always sings ä for ă because it is more artistic. Great care was used in such self-evident words as händ and änd but under the stress of enthusiastic interpretation, the exponent of ä for ă actually used seventeen pure ă vowels in one verse of one English song. Conversational muscle habits were stronger than artistic (?) intentions.

This "hahnd" and "ahnd" stuff not only disgusts the author—in good college slang it "gives him a pain," for it changes meanings in such a ridiculous way. Had becomes a hod carrier, sad becomes a piece of sod, the flag becomes a flog, your hat gets hot, sap turns into sop, and a slap is slop. Sometimes it becomes sacrilegious like the soprano whose "Lord mighty in battle" came out "The Lord mighty in bottle." Suffice it to say that we should learn to sing all vowels resonantly and beautifully if we are to appear normal and intelligible to our audience.

The diphthong ou in the third syllable of this group should be sung as a pure ä vowel, using the ōō as a vanish just preceding the s in sĭ. Advantage should be taken of the muscle feel of the vanishing ōō to assist in maintaining full resonance in the ĭ vowel, for the breathy s and small ĭ have a strong tendency toward oralization. The following through of abdominal lift is very essential in this group. Without that support, the final syllable, sĭ, may take advantage of the breathy s and produce a breathy ĭ vowel.

Group IV

pû   as in pull
gô   as in gone (American midwestern gawn)
vē   as in veal
rōō   as in room

In the fourth group, except for the ô vowel, the group consists of very small vowels. If one will look in the mirror while pronouncing this group, he will notice that he scarcely parts his teeth on pû, vē, rōō. This group is generally the most difficult in which to maintain full resonant beauty. The breathy p may cause the û to turn breathy, the small ē may become tense and oralized, the throaty r may destroy all freedom of resonation for the ōō. The r consonant creates a problem of its own. After all the author's insistence that pronunciation for singing should be the same as cultured speech, the *r* consonant is the one exception. The common pronunciation of *r* used in America (the tongue pulled back from the teeth and tensed) cannot be used artistically either as a consonant or a vowel, for its muscle interference blocks its vowel use and is too slow for consonantal speed in blending. Voice teachers have solved its interference by using the French or Italian trilled form for singing purposes. This trilled form is most easily acquired by practicing some phrase like "'Round the rough rock the ragged rascal ran," rolling each *r* with a good vigorous roll with the tip of the tongue, and then through practice, cutting down the number of trills until a single flip of the tongue-tip can be used for either an initial or closing *r*. Several foreign languages also use a guttural *r* which to an English or American ear sounds like an *l* until one is trained to hear its velar quality. Nothing has ever struck the author as being any more humorous than hearing an Austrian Doctor lecturing at a meeting of the National Association of Teachers of Speech on muscle actions in pronunciation, remark with all seriousness, what sounded to the author's American ears like "Some Neg*l*o t*l*ibes have t*l*ouble diffe*l*entiating between *l* and *ä*." To an American ear he did not need to go to a "Negro tribe" for his "trouble."

This last group is very carefully arranged to assist the voice student to acquire full resonation. If the *p* is pronounced quickly, the *m*-hum will assist the *û* vowel to remain clear (see Exercise 5, Series II), the *gô* will assist the *vē* and the *vē* will influence the *rōō* toward freedom in muscular effort.

The student should notice that the *gô* syllable is used both in the large group of vowels (Group I) and in the extremely small group with the *pû, gô, vē, rōō* (Group IV). This is done purposely to show that both *ä* and *ô* (*aw*) are variable vowels. They are the only vowels which can be pronounced on many sizes as far as jaw and lips are concerned. All other vowels are very specific in size and shape and if distorted take on the form and quality of the next larger or smaller vowel. The *ä* and *ô* (*aw*) can be pronounced on many sizes and retain their normal quality, for the tongue can assume the proper distance from the roof of the mouth at almost any jaw position without much tension. The student must, however, study his own forms and see that no habits of distortion are allowed. If even the *ä* and *ô* are too much overstretched, they will take on the quality of muscle interference because it will force their articulation too far back in the mouth. If the forms are too small the *ä* will assume the quality of *ŭ* and the *ô* will become *ŏŏ*.

After one has acquired full resonation in the singing of these groups, the singing of songs with uniform tone quality and resonance, can be done with very little application work.

The fifth basic technique in voice emergence is the use of each individual's normal articulation habits through absolute freedom in jaw, tongue, and lip action, that the modifications of speech for singing may be carried on without muscle interference.

TONGUE EXERCISES

The 19th Century, with Vaccai,[9] Concone,[10] Sieber,[11] and Marchesi[12] might be called the century of emphasis on training the intrinsic muscles of the larynx. Literally thousands of vocalises were written and used for developing the flexibility and speed of the muscles of the pitch mechanism with almost a total neglect of the muscles of articulation. In fact, the use of the Italian ä, without consonants, as the principle vocalizing medium, avoided articulation. Problems of articulation are mainly problems of tongue flexibility.

In infancy the human tongue has a normal position of great flexibility. From early infancy a baby constantly experiments with his tongue in the actions he uses in sucking and swallowing. Between the ages of four and nine months he discovers he can turn it over both ways. At least, to date, we have been unable to find one who doesn't. This flexibility is destroyed in a large percentage of people through habits of right-handed and left-handed chewing and swallowing, teeth extractions or tonsillectomies.

Many students have slow moving tongues that actually get in the way of normal actions. Some have such strong right-handed or left-handed chewing habits that one side of the tongue is fairly anchored in the mouth. The writer has had some who could not even swing their heads to the opposite side from which they chew while singing a tone, without completely shutting off the vowel form. Some have had tonsillectomies that have left scar tissue which pulls on the muscles in front and in back of the tonsil pockets so that it interferes with the arching and lowering of the soft palate in its regulatory actions for resonation and pitch. Lack of ability to articulate freely while singing in the upper part of the range, and the whole system of vowel modification in the upper voice, is much more a result of this lost flexibility in the adult tongue than a problem of acoustics. All students need a flexibility in tongue actions which allows the overlapping and blending of consonant and vowel articulations to be done effortlessly and with great speed.

In a research, for the Dental Clinic of the University of Michigan,[13] running from 1946 to 1955, done by Drs. Wright, Muyskens, Strong, Westerman, Kingery, and Williams, several hundred subjects have been

---

9 Vaccai, Niccolo, 1790–1848, *Vocal Method.*

10 Concone, Guiseppe, 1810–1861, *160 Solfeggi* and *Vocal Studies.*

11 Sieber, Ferdinand, 1822–1895, Song, studies, vocalises, catalogue of 10,000 German songs.

12 Marchesi, Mathilde, 1826–1913, *Method.* Many sets of vocalises.

13 *A Study of the Tongue in Relation to Denture Stability.* Wright, Muyskens, Strong, Westerman, Kingery, Williams. J.A.D.A., September, 1949.

examined for chewing and swallowing habits. This investigation has not only fully verified the above findings, but has shown that the following tongue exercises are not only of inestimable worth in speech and singing but are invaluable in the stabilization of lower dentures. Just as perfection in boxing demands full development of legs and upper torso through rope jumping and bag punching; in violin and piano playing, a careful development of the muscles of the fingers; so the singer needs development in the freedom of the muscle actions of articulation as well as those of the pitch mechanism.

The following exercises will give flexibility to stubborn, interfering tongue muscles. If taken twice daily for a period of six weeks, repeating each exercise rapidly many times, the most untractable tongue will become flexible.

1. Run the tongue out and in as rapidly as possible, flipping the tip as in the pronunciation of *l* as it darts back and forth.

2. Move it rapidly from side to side, with the tip extended far enough so that it hits the sides of the lips.

3. Open the mouth wide as in yawning; vigorously extend the tongue out of the mouth as far as possible, jerking it back to its farthest position. One will find that the lips assume a smiling position on the extension and an $\overline{oo}$ position when it is jerked back.

4. Turn the tongue over, so that the right edge is on the left side of the mouth, reversing quickly so that the left edge is on the right side of the mouth. This exercise is very difficult. Most students can turn the tongue over one way, but not the other. It is, however, the most efficient exercise of the group for increasing flexibility when the ability to do it is acquired. Many find it easy to turn toward the side they use for chewing, but difficult to turn away from that side. A mirror and patience will turn the trick.

5. With the mouth open, silently pronounce *gŭ*, until by raising and lowering the root of the tongue vigorously, one can form a complete groove down its full length. Be sure that this action is one of raising and lowering the back of the tongue and not moving the tongue forward and backward.

6. Pronounce "$\overline{ee}$yŭh". Produce the $\overline{ee}$ pianissimo on the very highest pitch possible, breaking it open with a vigorous jaw action on the spoken *yŭh*. This throws all the musculatures of an open throat into a vigorous action stronger than used in singing high pitches. In some students the pitch which breaks through on the $\overline{ee}$ vowel is within a perfect fifth of the top of the keyboard.

These exercises are invaluable for warming up the throat and loosening accumulations of phlegm early in the day. Combined with the humming exercises of Series I, and the drinking of a great deal of water, they will eradicate most incipient colds and sore throats.

RESUMÈ

Before beginning a discussion of specific techniques for practice in vocalizing we should once again think through the framework of voice emergence and in the simplest possible form bring to our minds the techniques which make posture, respiration, phonation, resonation, and articulation blend into the single unit of a beautiful, flexible, and resonant voice.

The basic technique in RESPIRATION is an alert and erect posture to free the flexible use of diaphragm descent and abdominal lift.

The basic technique in PHONATION is an erect head position to free the flexible use of the pitch mechanism for clear tone production.

The basic technique in RESONATION is the flexible use of an open nasal port.

The basic technique in ARTICULATION is free and flexible jaw action to release an easy rapidity in tongue and lip muscle movements.

SERIES I

CHAPTER VII

HUMMING

W HEN the voice teaching profession acquires enough knowledge concerning all the physiological details of the emergence of the human voice in the framework of posture, respiration, phonation, resonation, and articulation, then anyone with a normal physiological equipment can be taught to sing beautifully.

The basic need is for simple techniques to assist in the overlapping and blending of as many sets of musculatures used in that emergence, as is possible. The use of the pianissimo *m*-hum in early vocalizing supplies such a basic need. This is true because it develops the co-ordinated use of the first four of the five fundamental techniques. If the *m*-hum is produced *free from muscle interference* and *fully resonated,* good posture will be assisting respiration, abdominal lift will be assisting clear tone production, and clear tone will be assisting resonation activities. Only the complications of articulation are left out of the humming act when an *m*-hum is used.

All infants sing before they speak. In fact, the God-given acts of singing are used for speech development. The infant hums while he nurses or when he lies full and contented in his cradle. This little grunting hum keeps milk from getting into the wind pipe. It has definite pitch. This humming pitch of nursing infants has been recorded from G above middle C to B♮ below middle C. In fact, the author's grandson flatted a half step when he was full, satisfied, and lazily content but still nursing. The same action in later life becomes our colloquial yes— "m-hm," and prolonged, becomes the accepted exclamation for a mouthful of tasty food—"m-m̂." It also becomes our colloquial "no" when used with a double accent "m̂-m̂." The letter "m" is the sign for it. Approximately 21,000 words in English begin with it, about 7,000 begin with the "n" hum, while no words in English begin with the "ng" hum.

In the Chapter on Resonation we have seen how research in acoustics bears out the concept that the muscle positioning of the pianissimo *m*-hum is an optimum position of the throat, soft palate, uvula and tongue, for freedom in resonation. The *n* uses muscular activity with the tip of the tongue against the gums above the teeth and *ng* uses the muscular activity of the body of the tongue against the roof of the mouth.

By the time we reach adult life we have developed twelve easily distinguishable hums. Each of the three forms of *m, n,* and *ng,* may be produced four different ways: clear; breathy; with tensions in the muscles of the floor of the mouth; or with the muscles of the walls of the pharynx squeezed.

The *clear* type of hum is produced by closed vocal lips as in Illustrations E, F, and G of Plate III. It is easily distinguished by its resonant purity and its muscle feel of complete freedom in production, with the sense of balanced poise from the abdominal lift to the tones vibrating in the bony structures above the level of the roof of the mouth.

The *breathy* or *falsetto* type is produced by slightly opened vocal lips as in Illustrations D and H of Plate III. The breathy hum, through failure of complete closure of the vocal lips, allows the breath to flow out of the nostrils in a rapid stream, the abdominal lift literally "caving in" through lack of breath pressure being built up at the vocal lips as in the clear hum when the vocal lips are closed.

The *tense floor of the mouth* hum is recognized by its reedy, clarinetlike quality and the fact that as the hum is attacked the muscles under the chin literally jump down with a tense thrust.

The *pharyngeal squeeze* is a partial closure caused by tension of the pharynx. Any constriction in the pharynx will produce tensions in the soft palate, root of the tongue and larynx. The pharyngeal squeeze is recognized instantly by its throaty quality. This quality is caused by the loss of the free transmission of the tone vibrations through the tissues and cavities to the bony structures surrounding the pharynx, naso-pharynx, nose and mouth.

In the clear hum, tone vibrations in the lower part of the range may be felt by placing the hand on the top of the head, the face, nose, chin, throat, chest, or the back of the neck. The vibrations seem to be leaving the body from every direction. All the membranes of the pharynx, nasopharynx, nose, and mouth have transmitted the vibrations to the sinuses and bony structures. If the hum is a true *m*, without tongue interference, it will burst from the lips when the lower lip is plucked and one will actually hear the pitch in the lip membrane. This clear *m*-hum seems to leave the body so freely and fill any room or auditorium so completely that the listener cannot locate its origin. The hum produced with the pharyngeal squeeze is so localized in its resonation that the listener hears it as emanating directly from the tight muscles squeezing the pharynx.

An analysis of the *m, n,* and *ng* in muscle actions shows that the *m*-hum is far superior to the other two in helping to build freedom in resonation. The *ng* closes off the entire mouth where over 99 per cent of articulation takes place, and also forms the habit of a raised interfering tongue and tense muscles in the palate. Constant use of an *ng*-hum can only result in nasal twang or muscle interference. It also tends toward the use of the pharyngeal squeeze instead of clear production. Although fine and beautiful in quality, the *n*-hum blocks the front of the mouth, with the raised tip of the tongue, where over 85 per cent of the English language is articulated. The *m*-hum forms a perfect condition for a vocalizing technique. There is no articulation contraction. The tongue lies lax in the mouth in the neutral vowel position. Vibrations of the pitch tone, produced at the vocal lips, have free access to pharynx, nasopharynx, nose, and mouth without any muscle interference. These vibrations are transmitted freely through the membranes and muscles of the vocal tract, into the complete bony structure of chest, neck, and head until the whole structure from chest upward is one vibrant instrument.

If the singer has a keen sense of tone vibration transmission, he may feel a concentration of vibrations around the area of the front upper roof of mouth and lips. The cause of this sensation is the amount of vibration in the nasopharynx, nose, and mouth which makes the hard palate and upper teeth vibrate vigorously. This vibration sense at the lips is strongest for most students in the middle lower part of the range. It leaves the lips, and rises into the bony structures surrounding the cavities of the nasopharynx and nose in the upper voice. This shifting sense of vibration transmission is caused by the arching of the soft palate which occurs on high pitches as part of the muscle action in positioning the larynx.

The author's investigations in fundamental and overtone resonation showed that the pure *m*-hum was so strong in fundamental tone, that sometimes a reading glass was necessary to distinguish the upper partials in the wave form. This strength of fundamental makes the *m*-hum as a technique, of incalculable worth in voice emergence, for the universal fault of beginning students is too much oralization (use of the mouth), with its attendant harsh, strident quality, and strain on the pitch mechanism. We have seen in the chapter on *Resonation* that this strident quality is caused by too much reinforcement of the overtones of vowel forms, and not enough strength in the resonation of the fundamental pitch tone on which the vowel form is being sung. The muscle habits developed through vocalizing with the *m*-hum produce the necessary strength in fundamental resonation and the strident quality becomes the thrilling edge of a beautifully resonant tone.

In the chapter on Phonation, we have seen that the colloquial affirmative, "*m-hm*," gives us the technique for judging the emergence of a clear *m*-hum. The author has yet to find a student who uses a breathy tone production on the spoken *m-hm*. The first half of the expression is a clear *m*-hum started from closed vocal lips. The second half, *hm,* is a clear *m*-hum started with open vocal lips, coming to a complete closure after the *h* consonant. Either the *m* or *hm* can be used as the initial technique for clear tone emergence. The writer prefers the *m*

(not the letter *ĕm,* but its sound) as it forms the habit of clear tone
from closed vocal lip position, giving one the chance to check for any
tendency toward prominence of glottal catch and to learn attack and
release by abdominal lift as the sole source of the energy surge for
building the breath pressure for singing.

There are certain rules that the pupil must observe if humming is to
be a real asset in his vocal training:

1. Do not hum loudly in the upper part of the range, for powerful humming in the upper range tends toward throat constriction.

2. As one hums higher in the range, the hum should grow lighter and
more flute-like and have the feeling of leaving the lips in favor of transmission in the cavities and structures above the roof of the mouth. This will
occur with altos and basses at about B♮ or C, with mezzos and baritones at
C♯ or D, and with sopranos and tenors at E♭, E♮, or F, these being the
pitches where the arching of the soft palate becomes strong enough to make
one feel a shift in vibration transmission.

3. Never hum below that part of the range in which the hum stays clear,
for breathy tones injure vocal folds.

4. Never hum in any part of the range, heavier than the volume necessary
for sensing complete and free resonation.

5. A wise precept for humming as a basic technique is that it should always
be PIANISSIMO, PIANISSIMO *pianissimo* pianissimo and still retain vitality.

Humming has three functions: to teach a clear tone, to train the
opening of the nasal port, and to allow each student to examine carefully and accurately his own feelings of resonation (not his teacher's)
on every pitch of his range. To use it to the detriment of any of those
functions is to destroy its purpose.

SERIES I

The exercises of Series I are designed for three purposes. First, by
the smallness of the range involved, they give the student the opportunity of developing a free use of full resonance, without interference
from pitch consciousness. Second, by their simplicity, they allow him
to check his breath control techniques as he works, and firmly fix
correct posture and breathing habits before starting open vowel work
involving concentration on other vocal problems. Third, they acquaint
him with the principle melodic figures and diatonic cadences used
around the tonic.

The student should speak the closed-lip *m* several times to insure a
breathless hum. Then start near the center of his range with *Exercise 1*
of this first Series and proceed by half steps downward as long as he can
keep the tone breathless, flute-like, free from interference, and without
feeling any tension in the muscles of the jaw, tongue, lips, or throat.
Start *Exercise 2* in the middle of the range, proceed upward by half

steps as long as the tone remains breathless. The rest of the Series increases the range involved. *Exercise 3* proceeding downward, *Exercise 4* proceeding upward, *Exercise 5* proceeding downward and *Exercise 6* proceeding upward. *Exercise 7,* which is No. 1 in the permanent Series, proceeds upward.

Exercise 8 needs special explanation, for it is not only the closing exercise of the humming Series but is also a special exercise designed for the development of the lower part of the student's range. It is especially adapted to extending the lower range of bass and alto voices. The first two turns are a regular resonant hum, but an *h* is snuffed before the hum on the dominant below and the tone is slurred upward to the tonic. The exercise is continued downward by half steps as long as the student can feel the *breath pressure suspension* of the abdominal lift following the snuffed *h*. When the tone on the dominant becomes the least bit breathy, the exercise should be started again from the center of the range, proceeding downward as before. Most voices will add several half tones by the use of this exercise and the lower part of the range will become firm and resonant. The student must not use force on the exercise, but seek a balance between breath control and closed vocal lips. The slower the pitch vibrations, the lazier the controls become. The old empirical finding must be kept constantly in mind, that "Humming should be as easy as breathing."

This first Series may be abandoned after the second Series has been memorized, but the author's students constantly report that with the least suggestion of a cold they start their vocalizing with this first Series, for it clears the head and throat of interfering mucous and phlegm, creating a conscious freedom in resonance and lays the foundation for easy vocalizing of the permanent Series.

Although the clear *m*-hum, without muscle interference, is the most efficient as a voice building technique and is the only hum which should be used for vocalizing purposes, there are innumerable types of humming which can be used for choral effects. They include the *m*-hum, the *n*-hum, the *ng*-hum, the clear hum, the breathy hum, the muscle-blocked hum (some seven varieties of muscle blocks making qualities from English horn to bassoon) and finally the clear *m*-hum with the inside of the mouth shaped to all the vowel positions and diphthongs, *ē, ĭ, ā, ĕ, ă, ä, ô, ŭ, ō, o͝o; o͞o, ī, au, oi, ū*. The choral conductor has not yet scratched the surface of possibilities of choral effects by humming. One of the author's favorite humming techniques with familiar old folk songs is to say to the choral group, "Say the words to yourself as you hum, being sure that the accent, rhythm, and natural word feel of your energy surges are as if you were speaking the words." An audience can actually follow the words of familiar songs when hummed with this technique.

Throughout the history of voice teaching, there has been a recognition of the need for developing the so-called "head voice." In reality the "head voice" is *nasalization* and the greatest source of its development is through the technique of an *m*-hum. *Nasalization,* or tone vibrations passing freely above the roof of the mouth as well as into the mouth, is caused by the use of the *open nasal port.* The *m*-hum is the physiological technique which patterns and conditions that opening. The vocal student must never confuse *nasalization* with *nasal twang.* *Nasalization* is beauty through freedom of resonation of all cavities and bony structures above the roof of the mouth, strengthening the fundamental tone. It has already been stated in Chapter V that *nasal twang* is the disagreeable quality caused by *blocking* of the nasal passages. This blocking may be produced in many ways: by pinching the nostrils; a bad cold; adenoids; a broken nose; a deviated septum; the back of the tongue being raised and partially closing the nasal port as in the pronunciation of *ng.* The quality of *nasal twang* in the human voice is *always* caused by the blocking of the nasal passages, *not their free use.* Even the nasal twang of cleft palate cases is caused by blocking at the nostrils, the nostrils not being large enough to emit the abnormal number of vibrations concentrated there.

The author's recent investigations in the effect of nasalization upon the relative strength of fundamental and overtones in the tone wave form, show the worth of the muscle pattern of the *m*-hum in the emergence of beautiful tone. Through its use, one may eradicate the shrill blatancy of too much oralization, conquer the muscle blocks of so-called "coverage," and acquire the strength of fundamental resonance which is recognized as the "resonant line" in all great artists.

The problem of developing the so-called *head voice* (see Plate III, Page 27. Ill. G and H) is generally simplified by the use of the pianissimo *m*-hum as a vocalizing technique. It makes each individual aware of his personal sensations of reverberation and resonance through the transition into the upper part of his range. This eradicates the necessity of so-called *coverage,* which all too often is merely a name for muscle interference through the transitional pitches. With the use of the pianissimo *m*-hum muscle pattern and its attendant sensations as a criterion for emergence of a free tone in that c♯ d, d♯ e transitional spot, baritones who believed that one should sing with a closed nasal port, find their lifelong problem solved. Sometimes this occurs in less than six weeks.

A clear, delicate, and refined *m*-hum builds a range of unbelievable length (in many individuals between three and four octaves) and is the basis of the easy, quick, and sure development of unusual flexibility and power.

The teacher or student, who does not use humming as a basic technique for voice development, is throwing away the simplicity of the God-given approach to speech and singing used by the entire human race in infancy. The *m*-hum also provides one of the surest means of recovery of damaged voices.

The pianissimo *m*-hum is the basic technique for the overlapping and blending of the musculatures of posture, respiration, phonation, and resonation.

SERIES II

CHAPTER VIII

EXERCISES

JUST as the football, basketball, swimming, tennis, baseball, track, and golf coaches use certain exercises for the development of body co-ordination for their specific athletic activities, so the study of voice needs the use of vocalizing exercises to build the complete freedom of co-ordination in the overlapping and blending of the musculatures used in voice emergence.

Just as the football player must know the fundamentals of blocking and tackling and the tennis player of serving and volleying, so the voice student must build into his body the most efficient controls for respiration, phonation, resonation, and articulation. Just as the golf player must develop a keen sense of timing and distance for all strokes, so the vocalist must know his rhythmic pulses, his intervals, his scales. Just as the baseball player must be ready to spear a line drive or cover a slow rolling bunt, so the singer must be equipped for the production of powerful climaxes or delicate pianissimos. Just as the basketball player must be able to make his shots from any angle on the floor, so the vocalist must maintain a fully resonant tone on any pitch in his range, whatever the vowel or consonant combination.

Singing, the same as any other athletic work, is an act involving muscular control of the body. The freedom of the voice is in the freedom of those controls; the power of the voice is in the power of those controls; the delicate nuances of the voice are in the delicate nuances of those controls; the flexibility of the voice is in the flexibility of those controls; the speed of the voice is in the speed of those controls; the automatic spontaneity of the voice is in the automatic spontaneity of those controls; even the beauty of the voice is in the beautiful ease of those controls. When you listen to a singer, you hear the virile muscular actions of an athlete or the flabby muscles of sedentary ease.

No two voice students are alike; even "identical twins" are not identical. What is difficult for one student may be easy for the next. For instance, with most students the $\ddot{a}$ vowel is easiest to sing with free muscle action and full resonation, but with some, because of the shape of hard palate, soft palate, teeth, or jaw, muscle action for the production of the $\bar{e}$ or $\overline{oo}$ vowel may be more free than the $\ddot{a}$.

Nevertheless, whatever the individual tendencies are, every student must have his breath under perfect, balanced control; every student must form the habit of clear tones, not breathy ones; every student

must develop the use of the open nasal port to strengthen the fundamental tone resonance; every student must learn to sing with such freedom of resonation that he can keep a beautifully resonant tone through
any combination of consonants and vowels in articulation. All of these
must be easily blended into the rhythmic patterns, the melodic line, and
the dynamic stresses of the song to be sung.

Teachers have written and experimented with thousands of exercises, for the patterning and conditioning of these controls. Most voice
teachers start from the *end product* of some vowel which is comparatively easy for the student with whom they are working. From that
beginning they try to find exercises for that individual which they hope
will develop his voice. But working from effect (the vowel) to cause
(the basic controls), instead of from cause to effect, they spend three,
six, eight, or ten years trying to do the work which could have been
done in six months to a year by positive techniques emerging from
posture through to the tip of the tongue, built in favor of the student
as a *producer* instead of the teacher as a *listener*.

The reason for writing EMERGENT VOICE is to produce a text which
teaches one to think basically from cause to effect—from posture
through respiration, phonation, and resonation, to articulation—and not
to guess psychologically from the tone produced, back toward its source.

We have tried in the text of EMERGENT VOICE to keep from any
atmosphere of adverse criticism of any so-called "method of voice production" and will continue to do so, leaving such tirades for those who,
through lack of knowledge of the three fields of physiology, physics,
and psychology, become highly emotional over the rightness of what
they think is true, although they may have only one-sided information,
or empirical findings from a very limited experience. Once patterned
and conditioned into automatic use, the human body is a marvelous
instrument of expression, our slightest change of thought or emotion
reflecting in the voice. *If it is taught the right thing to do and the
easiest and most efficient way to do it,* it makes no difference what one
believes about it, the body will still do its work with the greatest ease
and efficiency. All the absurd ideas in the world from "find the
specific gravity of the tone in your body" through "color your
words, pink, red, yellow, and black" to "focus the tone about three feet
in front of your face" cannot keep the student from singing beautifully if his body is taught *the right things to do.*

*The mind cannot control the body efficiently until the body has
built efficient controls into the brain. The cycle from body to brain to
body, must be patterned and conditioned into automatic use before it
becomes an efficient tool of the mind.*

This physiological and psychological fact is just as true for singing
as it is for tennis or golf. The age-old sarcasm "Are you a musician
or a singer?" originated from instrumentalists recognizing this natural

law of body, brain, and mind, while a large percentage of vocalists tried to ignore it, thinking that their beautiful, natural voices were all they needed to be public performers.

Exercises, to be of real worth to the student, must build a balanced, flexible, co-ordinated use of the five sets of musculatures of posture, respiration, phonation, resonation, and articulation and weld them into the single unit we call the *human voice*. These exercises must be built with full recognition of the motor psychology of the individual. By that we mean that the correct muscle actions must be patterned and conditioned until they become automatic and can be forgotten in favor of the psychological interpretation of the thoughts, emotions, passions, and moods of the song. Once that patterning and conditioning has been done, then the individual can put his entire concentration on the interpretation of the poem or libretto, for the singing tract is the respiratory tract and although every muscle of the respiratory tract is voluntary, the respiratory center of the medulla oblongata can take over all the acts of singing, when once patterned and conditioned, and use them as a completely involuntary mechanism.

The author has spent thirty years of careful work, sorting, sifting, and simplifying the exercises used by the voice teachers of the past and present, and has built a simple series of ten exercises which will develop the co-ordinated use of the musculatures used in the emergence of the voice from the body. They are arranged in such a way that they are progressive in freeing the muscular actions involved. They cover not only the problems of muscular activity, but interval progressions, articulation problems, and dynamics. Voice teachers, organists, choral directors, class voice teachers, and public school music teachers have declared them "foolproof" after seeing the results in resonant beauty from their use with both solo voices and ensembles.

These ten simplified exercises are based on the techniques discussed in the preceding chapters and will overlap and blend those techniques into a flexible, co-ordinated whole. They require but nine and a half minutes to perform. Anyone, with a normal physiological equipment, who will apply himself diligently to these exercises for a *minimum of three ten-minute periods daily* will very quickly develop a singing voice of wide range, flexibility, power, and beauty. The writer wishes to call attention to the fact that he said "three ten-minute periods" *not thirty minutes*. In other words, these exercises practiced three times daily at different times during the day, will allow the muscular controls used in their performance, to be rapidly patterned and conditioned into automatic use. In fact, the first five exercises alone, with special attention to the use of the *abdominal lift* as the energy surge in expiration controls, will completely co-ordinate the overlapping and blending of the five sets of musculatures used in posture, respiration, phonation, resonation, and articulation activities.

SERIES II

Exercise 1

[Before starting the first exercise of Series II, the student should review carefully the chapters on *Respiration* and *Humming*.]

Starting near the center of the range or a little below center for the initial pitch of the first tone of the five tone diatonic run, say the colloquial affirmative, *m-hm*, a few times. Place one hand on the abdominal wall at the soft triangle below the breastbone (sternum) between the floating ribs. Expand around the waist line. Speak a few light, dainty *m*'s (not *ĕm* but the sound *m* as in *mother*). Take a light catch-breath between each one. Feel the dainty inward and upward energy surge of the abdominal wall as the initial force of the *abdominal lift* builds up the breath pressure which produces the tone. Now hum a few tones using a pitch as near as possible to the initial pitch of the spoken *m*. Pluck the lower lip while humming, to find if the jaw, tongue, and throat are in the neutral *o͝o* position and the tongue free from the roof of the mouth. Listen and feel for any constriction about the larynx. A pure hum has no reedy quality in perception. It is pure fundamental tone, freely resonated. If a *pharyngeal squeeze* or the muscles of the floor of the mouth are used even slightly, the hum takes on the quality of the muscle blocking used in the constriction, and its free, pure, resonant quality is lost. The *pharyngeal squeeze* in humming is generally caused by confusing the dainty energy surge of the *abdominal lift* with the vigorous setting of the diaphragm against the strong tension of the abdominal wall used in the inverted breathing of those who bear down from above with expulsion controls.

Having identified the free, effortless *m*-hum, try the first exercise in the lower center of the range. If the slightest change of quality occurs, either the abdominal lift is not giving support with the ease and flexibility which it should, or the student has tensed some muscle action above the larynx which had nothing to do with the hum. Reread the last paragraph in the chapter on *Respiration* (page 23). Check the details of the *abdominal lift* and see that all actions involved in the humming are freely and flexibly balanced in their activity. One of the old Italian teachers used to say that "humming, correctly done, is as easy as breathing." Anyone following the instructions above and those in the chapter on *Humming* will find the truth of that empirical finding.

Exercise 1 is an *ascending* exercise and should be used as such. Our speaking habits have built into our controls two types of inflections—the rising inflection and falling cadence (of Exercise 1) and the falling and rising (of Exercise 2). Most readers will ask, "What do you *mean* by that?" and will use the rising inflection and falling cadence of Exercise 1, while some will ask, "*What* do you mean by *that?*" using the cadence line of Exercise 2. Constantly the speaking voice is rising and falling, or falling and rising as we make statements or ask questions. The falling cadence of the last half of Exercise 1 or the first half of Exercise 2 is the statement cadence of normal speech, while the rising inflection of the first half of Exercise 1 or the second half of Exercise 2 is the question inflection used in speech when we do not know the answer.

After trying Exercise 1 a few times in the Key of Bb, C, or Eb (depending on which key is the easiest to keep the hum *free in muscle action* and *uniform in quality*) proceed upward by half steps, repeating the exercise in each new key, as far as *muscle action remains free and flexible* and *quality of tone remains uniform*. (Of course, from *freedom of muscle action* there emerges a tone of *uniform quality*, so the expression *freedom of muscular action* and *uniform tone quality* are actually descriptions of the same thing—one cause, the other effect.)

If the student has a keen sense of tone transmission, he will feel, in the lower part of his range, a concentration of tone vibrations around the nostrils, spreading over the lips. The head of one of our great university conservatories who spent several years in Europe, studying voice with the best teachers of Italy, Germany, France, and England, reported to the writer, "Every worth-while teacher I had, claimed that he taught differently from anyone else, but every one of them used an *m*-hum as a basic technique and had me pluck my lower lip to be sure that the vibrations were completely filling my mouth."

The feeling of tone vibrations concentrated at the lips, shifts with the arching of the soft palate for high pitches. The student must always hum more softly as the pitch ascends. When one feels the tendency of the tone vibrations to leave the front of the mouth, teeth, and lips and seek a concentration above the soft palate in the cavities of the nasopharynx and nose, he should make no attempt in any way to maintain the sense of vibration at the front of the mouth. The shifting angle of the arch of the soft palate as the pitch ascends (caused by the ascending larynx) changes the location of the feeling of the vibration concentration, which rises into the bony structure of the head above the cavities of the nasopharynx and nose with the rising pitch. The actual location of this sense of vibration concentration varies with the varying shapes of pharynx, soft palate, tongue, teeth, jaw, and the arches of the roofs of mouths, as well as the pitch. It is the source of the so-called "voice placement" techniques. Freedom of muscle action for pitch production and resonation, account for this changing sense of the location of the vibration concentration (*not voice placement*). As the pitch ascends, the larynx moves up the throat.[1] The larynx and tongue bone are held in suspension by twenty-two muscles which assist in the raising and lowering of the voice box as it ascends and descends for high and

1 Secord, Arthur. *The Relationship of Thyroid and Cricoid Cartilages in High and Low Pitches*. Doctoral dissertation, University of Michigan, June 1941.

low pitches. When the abdominal lift is adequate and the resonation full and free, the feel of the muscles which hold the voice box in suspension is delicate and light. If breathing is inverted and resonation faulty, then the muscles assisting in raising the voice box for high pitches contract with such tensions that muscle blockings and throat interferences become very prominent. Tongue exercises 5 and 6 are invaluable in the strengthening of these musculatures.

After using Exercise 1, proceeding upward by half steps as far as the muscle actions are without blockings or tensions and the resulting quality is without the peculiar timbre caused by muscle blockings, proceed to Exercise 2.

Exercise 2

To start Exercise 2 use the *bottom note* of the last run sung in Exercise 1 as the starting point for the 5, 3, 1, 3, 5 of hum and proceed downward by half steps, using less and less abdominal lift, humming softer and softer, and using less and less effort in all muscle actions, going as far as the hum remains clear and breathless. Stop when the lower tones start to pick up the "crackling and frying" sound of mucous being torn from parting vocal lips.

The author wishes the student to notice that for every **ascending** *exercise there is a* **descending** *exercise. This is absolutely essential, for the muscular effort in the movements of the ascending larynx and soft palate in ascending exercises, needs the relaxation of a descending exercise to uniformly develop the complete range.*

These two exercises, welding the old familiar speaking inflections and cadences into the singing voice through careful co-ordination of the expiration controls of the abdominal lift, the clear hum of *m-hm,* and the arching and lowering of the soft palate in the high and low range, will accomplish very quickly the overlapping and blending of posture, respiration, phonation, and resonation controls. If the instructions as given are carefully followed, enormous ranges are quickly developed through the use of Exercises 1 and 2 only. Three octaves "as easy as breathing" are not at all unusual in the first month of training. The author has studying with him at the present writing, one coloratura soprano who hums, without the slightest constriction, over four octaves —from *G* to *a."'*

Humming *with any muscular interference* (which denies free resonation), *with any sense of effort* (except the slight feeling of the building up of breath pressure through the abdominal lift), or *with heavy tones in the upper or lower range,* or *with any feeling of throat constriction,* will retard range development.

The writer has purposely restated, in different language, many of the explanations already given in the chapter on *Humming,* for hum-

ming is the basic technique for blending the first four of the five muscular activities in the emergence of the human voice. By its correct use
both teacher and student have a positive, definite technique built in
favor of the student as a producer, applicable to all vocal techniques
and unbelievably quick in its co-ordination of posture, respiration,
phonation, and resonation for purposes of both speech and singing.

The common fault of almost every beginning voice student is a
harsh, shrillness of tone quality caused by too much oralization (mouth-
ing) of the tone vibrations emerging from the vocal lips. Exercises 1
and 2, by the muscle habits formed in the use of the open "nasal port"
(palatopharyngeal sphincter), give the foundation of correct muscle
habits for fully resonant tone. This building of positive techniques for
positive growth is the contribution of EMERGENT VOICE to voice training. Through their use, the teacher and student are not wasting months
and years of their time and energy trying to *correct faults* by "trial
and error" but are building positive habits of voice emergence.

One of the Middle West's best known vocal coaches, who is now
finishing his fiftieth year of successful voice teaching, remarked to the
author recently, "If I have learned anything from this half century
which would be of use to future voice teachers it would be two very
simple things: the teaching of a breath control adequate for taking
care of the demands of singing, and the building of enough resonance
above the roof of the mouth to make the tone beautiful." Every successful voice teacher becomes aware, empirically, of some of the simple
positive actions within the framework of voice emergence. EMERGENT
VOICE is concerned with positive techniques for the balanced, flexible
use of the musculatures of that *complete* framework.

The first two exercises of the second Series weld together the muscle
actions of posture, respiration, phonation, and resonation and pave the
way for practice in articulation with a freely resonated tone.

Exercises 3 and 4

Before the use of Exercises 3 and 4, the student and teacher should
review carefully and thoroughly the chapters on *Resonation* and *Articulation*. These two exercises are designed to show how freedom of
articulation has its source in freedom of resonation. Exercises 3 and 4
develop that emergence.

We have already seen in the chapter on *Articulation* that the *ä*
vowel is the largest and, with *ŭ* and *ŏŏ*, the most free of all the vowels
in muscle action. Unlike all the other vowels (except *ô*) the *ä* vowel
is *not* confined to one shape and size. It can be sung with great freedom
of jaw, tongue, lip, and throat position; however, too much overstretch-
ing will result in muscle blocking around the root of the tongue and too
little jaw action will change the *ä* to the *ŭ* vowel quality.

Exercises 3 and 4 are like 1 and 2 except that the jaw is dropped freely after the initial *m*-hum, and the exercises are sung on the repeated *ä* vowel as *mä-mä-mä-mä-mä*. To maintain the resonation activities of the *m*-hum in the articulation of the *ä* vowel the student needs only to add a freely moving jaw action (a vigorous chewing motion) to the *m*-hum. If this jaw action is not vigorous enough, the distance between the tongue and the roof of the mouth will produce the *o͝o* or *u͝* vowel but not the pure *ä*. (Refer to Plate VI for individual variations.) Concentration must be on the continuance of the freedom of the muscular action and vibration feel of the *m*-hum into the added *ä* formation. The more open the nasal port remains, the stronger will be the fundamental tone resonation and the less shrill the quality of an overemphasized *ä* vowel. *The open nasal port is merely the continuation of the muscle action and tone vibration feeling already established by the m-hum.* Do not try to open the nasal port.

In spite of its simplicity of accomplishment and its apparently easy, balanced, flexible, practically effortless controls, certain students will do every possible action of lips, tongue, jaw, soft palate, and throat except the simple one of dropping the jaw to the *ä* position. They may need to say *mŭm, mŭm, mŭm, mä* to find the normal jaw action *in themselves* for the pure *ä* vowel. Some students will completely close the nasal port when they open their mouths from the hum to the *ä* position, and will produce a harsh, blatant, oralized racket. Others will open the vocal lips when they open their mouths and turn the clear *m*-hum into a completely breathy *ä*. Others will squeeze the muscles of the throat and those around the tonsillar pocket (the pillars of the fauces) at the back of the tongue and sound as if they were singing into a bag of mush. Others will raise the back of the tongue against the soft palate in the *ng* position, partially close the nasal port, and produce the *ä* vowel with an exaggerated *nasal twang*. These four possibilities of changed muscle actions as well as their multiple combinations will never occur if the muscle habits of the *m*-hum as used in Exercises 1 and 2 are carried over into a simple emergence of the *ä* vowel through a freely moving jaw action *only*. In other words, *"Let the freedom of the muscle actions of the hum feed the vowel."*

One of the old Italian teachers once made the statement that it takes all the concentration and will power a student possesses to maintain the humming conditions of the nasal passages and throat when opening the mouth to sing. It does. Once the habit is formed of *maintaining the muscle pattern of the m-hum into the ä vowel*, the student has the complete framework of posture, respiration, phonation, resonation, and articulation patterned and conditioned, ready for use. Only when that cycle of muscle action of the *m*-hum into the *ä* vowel has been patterned and conditioned into automatic freedom, can one be sure that the many combinations involved in Exercise 5 will emerge with the ease and beauty necessary to artistic singing.

As Exercise 3 proceeds upward by half steps, the abdominal lift increases in vigor with the height of the pitch. One of the basic laws of sound is that every octave, doubling the vibration rate, demands nearly four times the intensity of effort if volume and quality are to be maintained. A steady, continuous, abdominal lift is particularly essential at that place in each individual's range where the larynx moves up the throat and the muscles of the soft palate arch to maintain the changing position of the larynx. An adequate abdominal lift combined with the full resonation developed by the muscle action patterned by the *m*-hum will completely bridge the so-called "register gaps" of untrained voices. [See chapter on *Resonation*.] This lack of co-ordination between the muscle actions of the middle and upper part of the range is especially prominent in basses and altos. In many individuals this lack of co-ordination is caused by the use of *muscle interference* in an attempt to create the ineptly described "dark tone" desired by altos and basses. This *muscle interference*, called "coverage" by teachers who do not understand the actions of *nasalization*, is the use of the muscles of the pillars of the fauces, soft palate, and pharynx for attempted resonation and consequent tone vibration absorption instead of the nasalization and tone vibration transmission of the open nasal port through the *m*-hum muscle pattern. Because of this improper use, the necessary arching of the soft palate, as the larynx moves up the throat for high pitches, is seriously hindered. Many basses and altos have come to the author for voice building, whose voices completely stopped at Db, D, or Eb, through the tensions caused by this muscle interference. When proper use of the abdominal lift and nasalization emerging from the delicate *m*-hum and diaphragmatic breathing, were built into their muscular controls, the upper voice developed quickly. Exercise 3 is practiced mezzo-forte that the student may consciously feel and adjust controls that are scarcely recognizable in pianissimo singing.

If the co-ordination of muscular actions remains free and flexible, the student will have the sensation of the throat and voice, opening into greater freedom and flexibility as the exercise mounts by half steps toward the upper part of the range. When any sense of tension or throat constriction occurs, *do not even try the exercise again,* but starting with the bottom note of the last run used in Exercise 3, use Exercise 4 as a relaxation exercise before returning to the upward progressions of Exercise 3. Except for the energy surges of the abdominal lift, singing should feel as effortless as maintaining one's posture. Any tensions destroy the beauty of the emerging voice.

Exercise 4 starts on the bottom note of the last run used in Exercise 3, proceeding downward by half steps. The tendency with most students is to oralize more and more as the pitch descends until the tone becomes a breathy, oralized, so-called "chesty" production. The student must concentrate in this exercise on less and less support in the abdominal lift as he proceeds downward by half steps, but for the lowest pitch of the exercise he must always use adequate support and sufficient nasalization to keep the tone from turning breathy. *The open nasal port is just as important on the lowest tone of the range as it is on the highest,* but the lowered larynx and the resulting lowered soft palate and larger throat position, with the natural vibration response in the larger cavities of the chest, very often deceive the individual into thinking that the resonation above the soft palate ceases to be important. *Less and less energy with more and more concentration on nasalization is the basis of growth of the lower range.* Never use the abdominal lift stronger than you have hum to match.

It makes no difference where in the range it occurs, the closure of the nasal port and the forcing of tone vibrations into the mouth cavity only (through tense muscle action), creates disagreeable tone quality. In the upper part of the range it results in shrill and blatant screaming and shouting; in the lower part of the range, in a raspy, chesty growl; in the center of the range, in a mouthy, throaty, forced blare.

As Exercise 4 proceeds downward, one finally comes to the place where the vocal lips no longer stay together and produce clean, clear puffs. When the quality of "crackling and frying" appears, resulting from mucous discharge slipping between the vibrating vocal lips, one should stop the downward progression. However, there are some basses, who, at the place where this "crackling and frying" occurs, open up a whole new section of the lower voice. A coarse heavy slow vibration appears. This slow vibration is the material from which so-called "Russion Basses" are built. Because the tone sounds like a motor boat on a lake, the author calls them "putt tones." They are not true tones but a division of the rate of the tone the bass thinks he is singing. Once developed, they add at least another octave, in perception, to the low bass voice. Oscillograph pictures of them show their rates becoming progressively slower until they become as slow as $4\frac{1}{2}$ vibrations per second as the bass superimposes their rates on the tone he thinks he is singing. While in perception they seem to be in the octave below low C they may be as low as the second octave below the keyboard. Once developed in the octave below low C they can be blended into the low voice, and down to C below low C they become the true "Russian Bass" tone. There is no injury to the upper voice from their free and simple use. The author has had one low bass who added a high G to his range during the year he developed his "putt tones." He has also had many reports from teachers using the simple exercises of EMERGENT VOICE, of their basses developing these tones of slow vibration rates. It is the author's experience that even the highest tenors and sopranos sing with perfect ease to the *F* below middle *C* with many of them developing a lovely resonant low *E♭* and some even the low *C*. A range of *c* to *f'''* is not unusual in both altos and sopranos when muscle co-ordination is free and flexible and the overlapping and blending of muscle action is without strain. Quality of voice and the part of the range in which one sings the easiest (the *tessitura* of the voice), determines whether one is a soprano, a mezzo, or a contralto—not vocalizing range. Vocalizing ranges may be identical in a high lyric soprano, and a contralto (this is true in the case of the two girls to whom this text is dedicated), but their easiest singing range varies greatly.

Even if only these first four exercises are used until the controls become automatic in action, an enormous difference in resonant beauty will show in both solo and group voices in a comparatively short time. From these first four exercises, however, voices may become so resonant that articulation becomes literally "covered up" by resonant beauty, unless the student or group are trained carefully in distinct articulation habits through the emergence of precise and accurate articulation by the use of Exercise 5.

Exercise 5

Before Exercise 5 is used, the student and teacher should review carefully the complete chapter on *Articulation*. Then starting with Group I (page 64) practice each group in minute detail for full and free resonation, studying and applying the principles described in the succeeding pages of that chapter. The use of Exercise 5 is the basic means by which the articulation of cultured speech can emerge into the singing voice. Once the muscle actions involved in the pronunciation of these four groups of syllables have become so automatic that resonation can emerge into articulation, the student is ready for folk song literature.

If the first four exercises have not fully developed the habit of the open nasal port, with its resultant full resonation of the fundamental tone, old habits of oralization will cause constant shifting of the balance of resonation above and below the roof of the mouth. Too much oralization will show in *thĕ, shă, sĭ, vē,* and *tā,* with resultant shrill, blatant harshness of tone quality, unless the *muscle and vibration feel* of the *m*-hum remains intact while the syllables are sung. The pressure built by the abdominal lift must hold firm, with a feeling of buoyant balance of control, or the tone will turn breathy after the breathy consonants *p, sh, s, t,* and sometimes even on the voiced *th*.

Just as it was essential for the muscle feeling and tone vibration concentration of the *m*-hum to remain intact when the student started practicing the *mä* syllable, so that same full resonation sense must be trained to emerge into the articulation of the four groups of phonetic syllables.

Exercise 5 is practiced slowly, with constant concentration on the techniques that develop clear tone and full resonation. Exercise 5 is used only around the center of the range of the speaking voice. This means that the *d′* and *g′* of Exercise 5 are for group or choral usage. In solo voices, altos and basses sometimes need its use as low as *b♭* and *e♭′*, tenors and sopranos as high as *g′* and *c′*. It should always be used on the interval of the perfect fourth, for the exercises of EMERGENT VOICE are not only building voice controls but interval recognition for the voice student. Exercise 5 purposely adds the perfect fourth to the diatonic five-tone scale and major triad already practiced in Exercises 1, 2, 3, and 4.

These first five exercises constitute the basic techniques for the emergence of the speaking voice into the singing voice. When the principles and techniques of EMERGENT VOICE are developed into automatic use by the concentrated practice of these exercises, the voice student will be singing freely, resonantly, clearly, and effortlessly. He will be capable of singing practically all folk literature. His tone quality will be his own. His articulation will be his own. His voice will be on the road to a flexibility in interpretation which the succeeding five exercises will quickly develop.

The second five exercises of EMERGENT VOICE are planned to develop in the voice student, flexibility, range, power, changing dynamics, and quick interval perception and to make automatic the energy surges of longer intervals and greater changes of stress and dynamics.

Exercise 6

Exercise 6 takes the tonic and subdominant triads and the dominant seventh chord line and makes them into a simple melodic phrase (1 ⟋ 3 ⟋ 5 ⟍ 3 ⟍ 1 ⟋ 4 ⟋ 6 ⟍ 4 ⟍ 1 ⟋ 3 ⟋ 5 ⟍ 4 ⟍ 2 ⟍ 7 ⟋ 1). It is well for the teacher to let the student or group sing some old folk song or a Stephen Foster song like "Old Black Joe" and let them discover that the tonic, subdominant, and dominant seventh chord lines are the foundation of folk song literature, playing the chords with them as they sing.

Exercise 6 should be done *very rapidly and delicately,* with concentration on the transfer of the *m*-hum *muscle and vibration feel* into the first *lä* syllable. By substituting Groups II, III, and IV, Page 64, for Group I, this exercise will serve the triple purpose of acquainting the pupil with the major triads in melodic form, of building rapid flexibility in pianissimo singing, and of giving him practice in rapid articulation. Jaw and tongue actions are synchronized. The old technique of dropping the jaw to a set position and flipping the tongue in the singing of the *lä* syllable is a false technique. If any individual will watch himself in a mirror as he speaks, he will see that jaw action constantly is used to release freedom in tongue action. This is one of the basic laws in the emergence of sucking, chewing, and swallowing, into speech. It should not be forsaken in the emergence of speech into singing. The author used the dropped jaw position and the flipping tongue for fifteen years in his own teaching experience. Since his research he has found that the synchronized jaw and tongue actions release normal freedom in articulation much more quickly than the dropped jaw position. It allows normal speech habits to emerge into singing habits in a natural way.

In spite of the fact that Exercise 6 is done softly and rapidly, the student will find that the abdominal lift is as essential as ever in carrying the feeling of nasalized tone vibrations into the upper part of the range.

Exercise 7

One of the quickest ways to find freedom in the resonation of climaxes in a song is to hum pianissimo on the pitch on which the word is to be sung, then speak the word from that pitch, leaving the humming muscle pattern intact. When asked to do this, a large percentage of students will hum the pitch, then speak at the pitch of their own speaking voice. This makes it necessary to teach students to speak from pitches.

Exercise 7 will do this very quickly. Starting on the bottom pitch of the last run of the upward progressing Exercise 6, let the student sing a pianissimo *m*-hum and use a spoken cadence on "la\ mi \no \ " and then sing the "go" on that pitch. Proceed downward by half steps changing the syllable group at each new pitch, speaking the first three syllables from the pitch and singing the last syllable each time as (speaking) "la\ the\ ta \ " (singing) "du—" etc., proceeding downward as long as the spoken cadence does not become the scratchy, fuzzy tone of the mixed clear-breathy production where breath exceeds the resonation of the initial hum.

Exercise 7 serves a double purpose. It not only teaches the student to speak from pitches, but lets him become aware of the energy surges of the abdominal wall in the spoken syllables. This serves as an essential preliminary exercise to the octave jumps of Exercise 8.

When transferring this exercise to song literature the procedure is to hum pianissimo on the pitch of the climax, then, by an inward energy surge of the abdominal wall *speak* the climactic word at full power. The student has the sensation of lifting through the pianissimo hum to full power on the vowel of the spoken word with all the muscular set-up of the pianissimo *m*-hum remaining intact. A hand on the abdominal wall, across the base of the soft triangle between the floating ribs, will show the energy used. Now sing the climactic phrase, with the hand on the abdominal wall, repeating the actions and sensations of the spoken technique.

Exercise 8

Just as Exercises 6 and 7 are designed for increasing flexibility and speed, Exercise 8 has for its main purpose, the development of power. All climaxes in singing are written in the upper part of the range. Practically all climaxes are reached by a leap of some interval varying from the minor third to over an octave—fourths, fifths, sixths, and octaves being the favorite intervals employed by most composers. This is perfectly natural, for the same intervals occur in increased emphasis of emotions and passions in spoken language. The ability to perform the octave jump with freedom and power is a basic technique in choral singing as well as in solo performance.

The ensuing instructions must be followed minutely if Exercise 8 is to perform its function of building power and freedom in the upper voice. The singer should always hum the octave softly as a preliminary exercise to singing the octave jump as it acquaints him with his own personal feel of the muscle action and resonation of the upper and lower pitch. If he uses the vigorous abdominal lift through the pianissimo hum to a powerfully spoken *mä* from the high pitch, as described in Exercise 7, he will have already sensed the muscle feel and resonation of the exercise when sung. He is now ready to practice singing the octave jump. The lower tone must be sung *softly* and *clearly* with full concentration on carrying over all possible *nasalization from the m-hum* into this light tone. Check for *abdominal lift suspension* to be sure the lower tone is clear. It may be well to say *mum, mum, mum, mum* softly and effortlessly on the lower pitch to be sure that full nasalization is present. A light, soft, clear tone, fully nasalized, on the lower pitch is absolutely necessary if the upper voice is to have complete freedom in an octave jump.

Concentrate on *resonation* (not on pitch) as a vigorous abdominal lift is used as the energy surge for the powerful upper octave. Be sure that this vigorous lift has a muscular feel of a direct continuation of the lower tone, not a new tone on the upper octave. If the nasal port is completely open and free on the lightly produced lower tone, the powerful abdominal lift will raise the voice box, open the throat, and arch the soft palate, and the upper octave will be produced with full power and freedom. There is a place in each individual's range as the octave jumps progress upward, where (because of the rising larynx and soft palate arching) the feel of the concentration of tone vibrations leaves the front of the face and rises higher in the bony structures of the head. This seems to be caused by the changed angle of the soft palate and the consequent change in the direction of the vibration transmission and concentration. The necessity of concentrating on resonation and not pitch in octave jumps is reflected in the old Italian saying, "When you sing up, sing down," just as the necessity of nasalization on the lowest tones of the range resulted in the old Italian empirical finding, "When you sing down, sing up."

When the slightest tendency toward throat tension appears in the upper octave do not attempt to go higher. In private practice, repeat the *mum, mum, mum, mum,* on the lower pitch a few times, then *speak* the pitch of the upper octave with the syllable *mä*, slurring from it with a spoken cadence of a full octave, as *mum, mum, mum, mum, MÄ* (1—1—1—1 ⁄ 8 ⧹ 1). Do this spoken octave slur several times, until the feeling of the muscle co-ordination necessary to its performance, is sensed. Become conscious of exactly how much abdominal lift is used in its performance. Now try singing the interval again. Very often, the ease of the spoken technique will transfer itself into the singing, and several half tones will be added to the range through the ease of its imitated actions. In a choral group, the instant one feels any tendencies toward muscle tensions he should reverse the octave, singing 8 ⧹ 1 ⁄ 2 ⁄ 3 ⁄ 4 ⁄ 5 ⁄ 6 ⁄ 7 ⁄ 8 with the *mä* syllable. When the run is reversed, the upper tone is done with power, the lower tone sung softly and power increased with the rising scale. In early rehearsals this reversed octave jumping is necessary with altos and basses or tensions would form through attempts to sing beyond the easiest range. It has been the author's experience that all low altos and basses can develop the octave jump as high as the high G which is as far as tenors and sopranos need to develop it. When the E, F, F♯, and G have been built into the upper voice with full power and freedom, the rest of the upper voice, in many students, will take care of itself. Very often, enthusiasm in interpretation will add a third to a fifth to the upper range of a voice freely produced.

The author wishes to re-emphasize the fact that in the octave jump there is no conscious change of any kind between the soft, light, clear, fully nasalized lower tone and the powerful, ringing freedom of the upper octave, except the change of resonation concentration rising in the bony structure of the head, resulting from the vigorous abdominal lift, which is the energy surge of the octave jump and automatically produces the changes of muscular actions necessary to its performance.

In private voice lessons, the writer uses the technique of the octave jump three different ways. First, humming before the lower pitch, then doing the exercise as described above. Second, humming the lower pitch and the upper pitch to check the feel of the resonation shift in the octave before doing the exercise. Third, humming the lower pitch, then the upper pitch, then speaking a vigorous "*mä*" in a normal spoken cadence from the upper pitch before proceeding with the exercise as described. The principle involved is that the student must develop an open nasal port and a recognition of his own resonation feels when making the octave jump. Different students sense the principle involved more quickly under one of the three approaches above. The student and teacher should check all three to find the one best suited to the individual.

Exercise 9

Exercises 9 and 10 are in complete contrast to Exercise 8. Their object is to build the necessary muscular controls for pianissimo singing.

Mezza-voce, or half-voice singing is absolutely essential in efficient interpretation. More than any other type of singing, it illustrates the principles of EMERGENT VOICE, for only by the most delicate overlapping and blending of muscular actions and a careful, flexible balance of controls can mezza-voce singing be done throughout the range.

Exercise 9, using the tonic chord line ascending and the dominant seventh chord line descending, shifting from *lä* to *rōo*, and *lä* to *vē*, serves three purposes—practice in mezza-voce singing, practice in the melodic line of the tonic and dominant seventh chords, and practice in articulation of the total vowel range—for the *ē*, *ä*, and *ōō* represent the extremes in muscular activity in vowel pronunciation.

Starting with the *m*-hum, following into the *lä* syllable, the soft mezza-voce tone is supported by a light, buoyant abdominal lift through the tonic chord line. A slightly added support is always given as the interval from 5 to 8 occurs and *is carried through to the end*. This is essential if muscle action remains free for the changing pronunciation from *lä* to *rōo* and *lä* to *vē*. When the *m*-hum resonation feeling is carried over into the *lä* and the slight energy surge is added at the syllable change, this exercise will have the flute-like ease of true mezza-voce. Starting in the Key of Bb or C it progresses upward by half steps to the Key of G or until the changing articulation of *lä-rōō* and *lä-vē* shows any muscular tension. Exercise 9 is always done so fast and delicately that the producer acquires an almost disembodied feeling about its production. The muscle feel of the soft *m*-hum seems to carry the whole exercise, and the jaw and tongue actions which do the pronouncing, seem to float along lightly, rapidly, and lazily below the feeling of the hum vibration concentration. Exercises 9 and 6 are similar for this delicate ease of performance.

Exercise 10

Exercise 10 is an exercise in true mezza-voce. Starting on *g''* it uses the minor third progression of 8 ↘ 7 ↘ 6 ↗ 7 ↗ 8 with the *lä* syllable, progressing downward by half steps to the bottom of the range. To initiate this exercise it may be necessary to start on the G' with a pianissimo hum and sing the *lä lä lä lä lä* to acquire the easy muscle feel of the hum pattern, then from B', then D'', then the high G. After this preliminary work to get the muscle and resonation feel of the exercise from the G'', *no humming is used in this exercise.* Even the lowest low-bass or alto can do it with the same ease as a soprano or tenor. It is effortless. To perform it with the ease for which it is designed, one must have complete freedom in the position of neck, head, throat, jaw, tongue, and lips, then letting jaw and tongue synchronize in the easiest possible manner, use just enough energy surge with the abdominal lift to set the thinned membrane of the vocal lips in vibration. In the early practice of this exercise, almost everyone will use many times the energy necessary and will produce a grunt but no tone. Sometimes it assists the student or group to find its easy emergence by trying it with a hum preceding it at *g'*, then *b'*, then *d''* and then *g''*. Sometimes basses and tenors will sing it with falsetto instead of a true mezza-voce. There is no objection to using falsetto, at first, as a substitute for mezza-voce. The only difference between the two, is that falsetto is breathy and cannot be increased to full power without pitch mechanism adjustment while the mezza-voce is sung with clear tone and can be used in a crescendo without a break. Many students will start Exercise 10 with a falsetto tone instead of a true mezza-voce but as the exercise proceeds downward by half steps it will develop into clear mezza-voce if one is constantly alert in the attempt to keep a very lightly balanced energy surge in the use of the abdominal lift with each new attack. This procedure will soon develop the true mezza-voce even in the attack of the *g''*. When done with the flute-like ease of true mezza-voce, it is capable of enormous range because of its easy, balanced, flexible muscle actions. It should start on *g''*; the amount of breath taken should be so little that one is scarcely aware of any expansion, the feeling being merely a relaxation of the abdominal wall in order to take hold with the abdominal lift to sing the *lä, lä, lä, lä, lä.* As the exercise moves downward by half steps to the bottom of the range, this light breath is taken between shifts to each new key. Being a practice in precise controls, it is essential that *a new breath be taken each time* the exercise is sung, even if the student feels that he could do many of them on one breath. This will give the student the practice of taking small, quick breaths for small, light phrases. As Exercise 10 proceeds down-wards by half steps, keep returning to the high G, leaping back from any pitch, even two octaves. This assists in eradicating falsetto and breathy tones and makes the true mezza-voce develop more quickly.

The writer has found that these ten exercises build the basic tech-niques necessary for practically any type of singing. After the student has built into his automatic controls, correct habits of pitch, quality, power, and articulation by the use of the exercises of Series II, then the songs he sings bring their definite problems of application in rhythms, melodic lines, phrasings, and interpretation. The glorious thing about the respiratory tract of the human body, however, is that once patterned and conditioned to automatic use, all controls can be forgotten in favor of the thoughts, emotions, passions, and moods of the song. Then the single unit of the emergent voice becomes a perfect tool of expression, controlled by the involuntary respiratory center.

A record of piano accompaniments for these exercises (all ranges) is available upon request to Hi-Fi Recording Studio, Box 62, Ann Arbor, Mich.

EMERGENT VOICE

SERIES III

SERIES III

The preceding exercises are for special problems of range extension, crescendo, decrescendo, and staccato practice.

The exercises of Series III are advanced exercises for increased flexibility and control. One could use literally hundreds of exercises in this advanced section, including trills, appoggiaturas, coloratura passages, and different types of rhythmical figures; but such vocalizing, really coming under the head of a study of musical theory, is not fundamental and should be studied, when it occurs, as a problem in the memorization of the music being performed.

For that reason, the closing exercises include only scale runs emphasizing the intervals of the 7th, 9th, and 11th, an exercise for practice in "messa di voce," three exercises in staccato singing, and an exercise in the minor, diminished, and augmented triads.

Voice work differs from all other instruments in that, when the voice itself becomes an instrument of beauty, flexibility, and power, the student has the ability vocally to perform music of practically any degree of difficulty. Sometimes this occurs in a few months of vocal study and the student finds his voice so far in advance of his knowledge of musical theory that his only opportunity of performing things, of which he is capable vocally, is through memorization by rote, with the aid of a competent coach. For this reason, the balance between skills, musical theory, and literature present a most puzzling problem in the field of voice education.

Exercises 1, 2, and 3 of Series III are for flexibility and range extension. They give the advantage of starting the initial hum in the lower part of the range while great height is being attained at the top of the run. In all of them the student must concentrate on nasalization of the first tone following the hum, watching that the feeling of the concentration of tone vibrations rises in the bony structures of the head identically with the feeling produced if the scale were sung with the hum only. A flexible jaw, a slightly increased vowel form as the top of the scale approaches, combined with an abdominal lift which follows through to the end of the phrase, will keep the tone pure and clear throughout the exercise. Drop the *mä* form in favor of the plain *ä* when the scale passes the G'' in range.

Exercise 4 is for practice on crescendo and decrescendo in the upper voice. It should start softly until the half note hold is sung, then increased from pianissimo to fortissimo and back to pianissimo on the half note hold and finished rapidly with a flute-like pianissimo.

The technique for the "messa di voce" is as follows: pianissimo, mezza-voce (half voice tones) always must be fully nasalized if muscle action is free enough to allow for the crescendo and decrescendo to be done smoothly. As the added support of abdominal lift increases the amplification of vibrations, the sound and **feeling** of the tone vibrations spread forward in resonation. At fortissimo all of the bony structures of the head above the level of the roof of the mouth vibrate with a brilliant ring, as the throat muscles increase their firmness to control the position of the larynx in response to the strength of the abdominal lift.

The decrescendo takes care of itself if the student merely stops increasing the support which he has at the height of the fortissimo, and holding that support, lets the tone diminish of its own volition by merely thinking the continued tone more nasalized as it decrescendos. On the turn following the "messa di voce" a slightly added support may be used again as the voice swings around the upper tone and finishes with the light, rapid run. This exercise may be used for the practice of crescendo only or decrescendo depending on the power of the attack on the dotted half note. The author's own experience in the use of the exercises of EMERGENT VOICE and also that of many teachers, whom he has trained, has been universal in the discovery that the ten exercises of Series II give all students the ability to crescendo and decrescendo at will without practice of any exercises for that purpose if the support of the abdominal wall is maintained during the decrescendo.

Exercise 5 is called the *ha, ha exercise* and is preliminary to the practice of staccato. It is merely the simple tonic chord line sung very rapidly with the syllable *hä*. Practiced with separate strokes of the abdominal lift for each syllable it makes a perfect preliminary exercise to all staccato singing.

Exercises 6, 7, 8, are for continued practice in staccato singing. Each of the staccato notes should be a unit in itself made by a quick, light, free stroke of the abdominal lift. Starting slowly and increasing the tempo of these exercises, a clear, clean staccato at vibrato rates can be acquired. It has been the author's experience that the ability to develop coloratura singing is exactly in proportion to a girl's athletic prowess, so his advice to all would-be coloraturas is that they had better become excellent swimmers, tennis players, ballet dancers, or acrobatic tumblers. There is a definite reason for this. These athletic sports develop the abdominal muscles to the necessary strength and speed for coloratura singing.

When the student has difficulty in singing diminished and augmented triads and intervals of modern music, a little regular practice with **Exercise 9** will bring a quick solution. This exercise completes the practice of intervals emphasized in Series II. It can be substituted for Exercise 6 of Series II, to show the intervals used in modern music as compared to the tonic, subdominant, and dominant seventh chord lines of folk song literature.

Once these advanced exercises are thoroughly mastered, the voice will emerge with such flexible and free controls that one's whole attention can be given to the interpretation of the poems in song literature and the voice will respond to the performer's slightest wish.

CHAPTER IX

DEVELOPING THE SPEAKING VOICE

There has been an enormous amount of literature on every aspect of public speaking and acting, but very little literature on *development* of the speaking voice. Just as the undeveloped singing voice is constantly in the way of the artistic interpretation of vocal literature, so the inadequate speaking voice is a constant handicap to the individual who wishes to impart knowledge convincingly.

To develop a voice with adequate dynamics, range, quality and durability; clear in articulation and pronunciation; and with projection capabilities equal to any situation; that is the problem faced by every individual who is called upon to speak publicly. The principles by which such a speaking voice is developed are identical with those for developing the singing voice.

The muscle actions of respiration which give the speaker his dynamics are identical with the singers.

The muscle actions of clear tone are the same for both.

The muscle actions which give the speaker *his* quality are identical with the singers.

The muscle actions of articulation are alike, except for duration.

In fact, the same musculatures of the respiratory tract are used for posture, respiration, phonation, resonation, and articulation in both the speaker and singer.

The student of speech would profit greatly in the understanding of his problems if he studied the text of EMERGENT VOICE in its entirety up to the chapter on Exercises, but the student whose main interest is in speech, should study most carefully the chapters on Singing and Speaking, Respiration, and Humming.

The tongue exercises at the end of Chapter VI are as essential to the developing of the speaking voice as they are in singing. In fact they are the God-given exercises by which the infant acquires the flexibility of tongue actions for use in articulation. They should be done a minimum of three times daily by the student of speech.

The prime objective of the student of speech should be the development of a voice of acceptable quality with adequate flexibility in power, range, and durability. All investigations in respiration have shown that diaphragmatic breathing with expiration support from the abdominal wall is the source of freedom in dynamic controls. Using these controls with pianissimo *m*-humming is the source of range, good quality and durability.

The transfer of power, range, quality and durability into the English language, with complete freedom in the dynamic energy surges of emphasis or accent, can be accomplished with a few simple exercises. Except for physical handicaps that interfere with the use of the musculatures of posture, respiration, phonation, resonation, and articulation, the only reason for failure in developing an excellent speaking voice is that the exercises involved are so simple that the student of speaking is apt to underestimate the worth of daily practice. Through routine of daily practice, right habits of speech must be built into the speaker's tissues until they are not only automatic but involuntary.

The power plant for the speaker, as it is for the singer, is in diaphragm descent for inspiration, and abdominal lift for expiration. This type of breathing, used involuntarily when we are sleeping or sitting and loafing and visiting with our friends, *must* become the breathing used in speaking if one fully develops his speaking voice. If you do not already use this breathing when speaking, acquire it. It is the most effective energy for your speech.

The next step to be determined is the pitch most effective for each speaker. The normal cadence at the end of a sentence involves a drop of a musical fifth. In order to provide room for this drop, *the average pitch of speech must be at least a major fifth above the lowest clear tone of the speaking or singing range.* This gives room for the falling cadence at the end of sentences without hitting "gravel." More potentially beautiful speaking voices have been ruined by the false concept that a low voice is beautiful, than by any other concept of either singing or speaking. When the expression "lower your voice" has been displaced with the concept of "put more hum in your voice" we will have beautiful voices, which *sound* low, at all ranges. The author has had the unique experience of having a student sent to him by a speech teacher because his voice "wasn't low enough." The voice was a constant, scratchy rattle from trying to speak below his lowest clear tone. The voice was raised *one entire octave* and trained for full resonation (full humming content) on every spoken word. In six weeks, the speech teacher who sent him, complimented him on how much "lower" his speaking voice was.

The effectiveness of the speaking voice is more in its resonation than its pitch. An example can be given by noting the wide range of pitches used by some well-known public speakers. Franklin D. Roosevelt used the pitch of A♭ below middle C as his basic pitch; Tom Dewey uses F below middle C; Dwight Eisenhower uses E♮ below middle C, while Herbert Hoover uses the C below middle C as his basic pitch. For accent purposes President Eisenhower's pitch moves up as high as middle C, but always carries with it a confident quality of assurance. Wendell Willkie, speaking without the muscle habits of humming in his voice, constantly tore the mucous from the edges of the vocal lips until the resulting raspy hoarseness caused his voice not to stand up under continuous use. The author, a high lyric tenor, speaks on middle C as his basic pitch with emphasis raising the pitch as high as a tenor's high G. Using any basic pitch below middle C does not leave room for a freely produced cadence at the end of sentences, and hoarseness results. *Humming content in the speaking voice produces a lower voice in perception when it may actually be higher in pitch.*

EXERCISES FOR DEVELOPING THE SPEAKING VOICE

Tongue exercises and the first four exercises of Series II of EMERGENT VOICE are the simple basic exercises used in developing a speaking voice. Add to them the six additional exercises given in this chapter and you will produce a fully resonant voice having a dark, rich quality.

Exercise 5

Use the four groups of English syllables of the **DYNAMIC PHONETICS** described in Chapter VI on Articulation, beginning on **Page 63,**

Hum on a pitch five diatonic tones up from the lowest clear tone of the range; take Group I of the English syllables "la, mi, no, go," speaking each syllable separately from that pitch. Most students will hum the pitch and then drop the voice to the lower pitch they have always used. See that the pitch of the hum and the muscle feel of the hum carries into the "la" syllable when spoken. After each separate syllable of the "la, mi, no, go," has been spoken from this basic pitch, speak the entire group with an energy surge (stress, accent, emphasis) on each succeeding syllable. Always hum on the basic pitch then say "la mi no go, la mi no go, la mi no go." Practice this both with separate syllables and each entire group with progressing energy surges through all four groups. This trains the speaker to bring out different meanings by shifting the emphasis: this trains the speaker, etc.; this trains the speaker to bring out different meanings, etc.; this trains the speaker to bring out different meanings by, etc.; this trains the speaker to bring out different meanings by shifting the emphasis.

Exercise 6

Starting two tones below the speaking pitch decided on in Exercise 5, use only the first syllable group with an energy surge on "mi." Repeating "la mi no go," let the "mi" rise higher in pitch on each repetition, through an energy surge from the abdominal wall, following the diatonic scale until the "mi" has reached a perfect fifth: "la mi no go, la mi no

1 2   1 1   1 3 1

go, la mi no go, la mi no go." After the fifth has been reached, then

1 1 4 1 1 1 5 1 1

begin to raise the perfect fifth interval one half tone with each repetition until the "mi" reaches a pitch where the resonation does not hold. The object of this exercise is to transfer the *m*-hum reverberation and muscle sensation into the "mi" syllable with an energy surge which can raise the pitch any interval up to a perfect fifth for emphasis, not only from the basic speaking pitch, but throughout the range.

Exercise 7

When Exercise 6 has reached its limit of upward progression and the "mi" starts to lose its humming content, use the pitch of the "la" in the final "la mi no go" and reverse the exercise "la mi no go," allow-

$$5 \quad 1 \quad 5 \quad 5$$

ing the "mi" to drop a perfect fifth. Take this exercise down one half tone with each repetition of the fifth downwards until the lowest limit of the range is reached.

Exercise 8

Starting again two tones below the basic pitch of Exercise 5, say the first two syllable groups in an upward progression "la mi no go la the ta du" ending with the emphasized "du" a perfect fifth above the starting point. Raise this exercise one half tone on each repetition until the limit of the range.

Exercise 9

Using the pitch of the syllable "la" in the final run of Exercise 8 run the "la mi no go la the ta du" down a perfect fifth. Lower this run one half tone on each repetition until the bottom of the range is reached.

Exercise 10

Professor Thomas Trueblood, the founder of the oratorical and speech department of the University of Michigan, insisted that a public speaker, to be most efficient, needed to know the use of "an octave twist" for emphasis. Starting at the lowest clear tone in the range carry Exercise 6 up to a full octave for emphasis: "la mi no go, la mi no go,

$$1 \quad 2 \quad 1 \quad 1 \quad 1 \quad 3 \quad 1 \quad 1$$

la mi no go, la mi no go, la mi no go, la mi no go" (the 1, 7, 1, 1, is

$$1 \quad 4 \quad 1 \quad 1 \quad 1 \quad 5 \quad 1 \quad 1 \quad 1 \quad 6 \quad 1 \quad 1 \quad 1 \quad 8 \quad 1 \quad 1$$

left out because of its disagreeable interval for speech). When the octave is reached move the octave up one half tone on each repetition until the upward limit of the range is reached.

These ten exercises done a minimum of three times daily will develop the speaking voice to a full power, range, flexibility, and quality in a comparatively short time. The actual time required will depend on such factors as the care in application of the student, previous habits contrary to freedom of speech, and the student's innate equipment.

These exercises with adequate added drill on problem consonants, are basic in correction of stuttering and speech defects, as well as the building of normal voices.

Chapter X

THEORY: BASIC RHYTHMS

THE most glorious voice in the world is of little use if its possessor is not well grounded in the fundamentals of good musicianship.

There is no excuse for any voice student stumbling on simple rhythms and melodic intervals when attempting to sight-read or memorize a new solo. If a vocalist wishes to have the joy of using his voice for either pleasure or profit, he must build a musicianship which will allow him to use it for reading rhythmic patterns accurately and for singing with sureness the intervals of melodies.

The three essentials of all music are *Rhythm, Melody,* and *Harmony.* They have developed in that order. The most uncivilized tribes of the world use only rhythm. As civilization advances, melody develops from rhythm. Only the more advanced civilizations have emerged from melody into harmony. One of the most marvelous developments in vocal music has been brought about by the addition of modern melody and harmony to the unusual and fascinating rhythms of the South African Negro through his contact with the music of the white man during his life of slavery in the southern United States. From this blending of melody and harmony with intricate rhythm, the Negro spiritual emerged. White man's fascination for these new rhythms brought forth the degrading forms of ragtime and jazz, and recently the development of swing has again blended melody and harmony with these syncopated rhythmic patterns. Now that some of our best composers are using their talent in this field, a completely new musical form is emerging which is as distinctive as any of those of the past.

It was the author's privilege to have charge of the music of the Negro drafted troops of Texas and Oklahoma during the first World War. It was practically impossible for them to sing many of the songs which the other soldiers used as their favorites, but every one of them could sing from memory about seventy-five Negro spirituals and work songs—singing in one rhythm, tapping their feet in another, and clapping their hands in a third. The most complicated rhythmic patterns man has ever conceived were easy and normal to thousands of Negro boys who could neither read nor write. A recent visit, by the author, to the Negro high schools of Dallas, Texas, showed such an amazing change in the last quarter century as to be unbelievable. The Negro principal of one of those high schools, a Ph.D. in Education, remarked that a new problem has arisen. This is to reconcile the new musical ideals of the

Negro high school choral members, singing beautiful artistic arrangements of eight-part Negro spirituals, with the hyper-religious emotionalism of their parents singing the same songs at prayer meetings and on Sunday. He finds it an almost impossible task. He saw no solution but the passing on of the older generation. The emergence of rhythm through melody into harmony in theoretical music is as fascinating as the emergence of the human voice from the crude vegetative actions of breathing, sucking, chewing, and swallowing through speech to singing.

If we are to approach our study of *Theory* from the causative angle as we did our *Skills* in singing, we must ask ourselves first the following questions: "What are the sources of man's rhythmic patterns? What are the normal rhythms by which the human race lives?"

Man only knows three rhythms: first, his heart beat; second, the nerve pulses that run his muscles; and third, his breathing. In the embryological growth of the human body, they develop in that order. Whole, half, quarter, eighth, sixteenth, thirty-second, sixty-fourth notes, and their multiple combinations are merely signs to represent these three rhythms and the patterns made by combining them.

Just as in singing most voice teachers have always taught from the tone back into the body, so in the teaching of theory of music, most teachers have always taught from the sign back to the rhythm instead of from the fundamental rhythm into the sign.

A note is *not* a sign one tries to translate into rhythms but is a sign to *represent* some natural, regular body rhythm. All the difficulties of teaching rhythm and time come from attempting to force these signs back into the body rhythms, instead of allowing the natural body rhythms of each individual to emerge into the sign.

The heart beat is the basic rhythmic pulse of the human body. It changes continuously with body activity, and the breath pulse and nerve pulses make most of their changes in relationship to it. When we are lying down, the heart beats on an average of about 66 to the minute. When we sit up, it rises to about 70. When we stand, it increases to about 80. Under moderate to heavy work, it speeds up to 150 or even 180 per minute. The Army Parade March, quick step, double time, and charge, are done at the average heart beats for those activities.

The rhythm of a band on the march is actually the rhythmic rate of the heart beat during the activity of walking. It is called *Common Time* because it is used more often than any other rhythmic pattern. Its 1, 2, 3, 4 is basic as a measure, as it is the natural number of steps taken to a breath by men when marching. Its sign is a capital C or the fraction $4/4$, which means that it has four quarter notes to a measure, the quarter note (♩) having been accepted as the sign in music to represent a heart beat. The heart beat may be as slow as in sleep and marked *Largo* or it may be as fast as the heart beat of a hundred-yard dash and marked *Prestissimo*. We can be sure of one thing and that is that man-made music is likely to remain within the limits of his own rhythms. It will probably never speed up to the rhythm of a mouse or canary, whose hearts beat as fast as over a thousand per minute, and it will probably never be as slow as an elephant's which is close to only twenty per minute.

Because of the varying heart beats of individuals we will always be thinking that so-and-so-'s rhythms are too fast and so-and-so's too slow. Probably the most basic fault of all music teachers is their constant attempt to impose their own rhythms on their students.

The proportion of heart beat to breathing rate is the true source of measure in music. Mowat's [1] investigations at the University of Michigan in 1940, showed a progressively slower breathing rate from youth to old age. In young children there are three beats to a breath. In youth it increases to a proportion of four to one. In adult life it continues to increase, but the basic feeling for three and four beats to the measure remains as the natural rhythmic rate for measure in music, the basic feeling of $\frac{2}{4}$ rhythm naturally coming from the feeling of two beats to inspiration and two beats to expiration of the normal breathing of youth.

This fundamental use of heart beat rhythm was recognized by the ancient Hatha Yoga health science of India, which taught its followers to work on their heart beat rhythm, and has been verified by Palmer [2] who found that the largest percentage of our natural accents in speech falls on the heart beat. If singing were taken away from the Negroes of the South, there would be mighty little work done south of Mason and Dixon's line. Almost every southern Negro works to the rhythm of his singing, and his singing is his heart beat.

For a period of three years, the author and Dr. Joseph E. Maddy, founder of the National Music Camp, co-operated in the broadcast of the Sunday Morning Hymn Sing of the University of Michigan. The author always felt that Dr. Maddy wished to rush the tempos, but both of us agreed that our accompanist always wished to play things much too slowly. The writer suggested that we take our pulses and check the fundamental difference. Dr. Maddy's was 86, the author's 72, and the accompanist's 64. Whatever the natural tempo of the hymn, fast or slow, the proportionate wish in tempo was always unconsciously based on those varying rates.

The next approach to reading the basic 1, 2, 3, 4 rhythm is to establish it in the body action of the student that he may express in a concrete rhythmic way this fundamental heart beat represented by the signs ♩♩ ♩♩. The most logical body action for him to use is the regular conductor's beat for ¼ or Common Time which is   and is

taught *down, across, out, up; down, across, out, up;*
tu, tu, tu, tu; tu, tu, tu, tu (pronounced as in *tuck*) using emphasis
on the first and third beat.

The syllable *tŭ* (as in *tuck*) is used by the author for all rhythmic
patterns because it is the fastest possible syllable in English, being
made up of the tip-tongue *t* and the neutral *ŭ* vowel. When rhythmic
pulses of the body are taught into the signs, and not the sign back
into the body, a simple syllable of this nature is all that is needed.
The ordinary method of counting with its *one andŭ two andŭ three
andŭ four andŭ* is complicated and unnecessary. In the rhythmic pattern of a conductor's beat, the voice student has the 1 2 3 4 or 1 2 3
expressed constantly in the conducting pattern which is more simple
to follow than the abstract counting which a singer can only do mentally
while his voice is being used for singing.

The following simple patterns are the fundamental patterns used
most in Common, ¼, or march time. They should be done first as single
measure rhythms, *tu, tu, tu*'d with a conductor's beat. Each measure
should be done over and over until its pattern is firmly fixed in the
student's body and mind. When this is accomplished, these measures
should be written out in phrases of four measures in many combinations
and then drilled as four-measure phrases. This type of practice is
invaluable for it sets the ability to read rhythmic patterns at a glance
by the normal process of the body to the sign until the reverse process
of the sign to the body becomes automatic.

This practice is done with the spoken voice at the pitch of C, E, G,
or B♭ depending on the natural range of the individual's speaking voice.
While transferring the normal body rhythms into the written sign, until
the written sign is instantly reflected in the responding body rhythm,
the student should not be bothered with melodic reading. The rhythmic
patterns should emerge into melodic reading after this fundamental
work has become automatic.

The first exercise is written out in full to show the initial use of
the spoken *tu, tu, tu, tu* in relationship to the conductor's beat and
the signs which represent these body energy surges in music. The staff,
made up of five lines and four spaces, is used with the signs written
on the pitch of G. This exercise is of one measure in ¼ time. It shows
the sign for the full measure (the whole note), and the signs dividing
that measure into halves (the half note), quarters (the quarter note),
eighths (the eighth note), and sixteenths (the sixteenth note). Above
the measure is the conductor's beat. Below the measure are the *tu-tu*'s
representing the rhythm.

Exercise 1

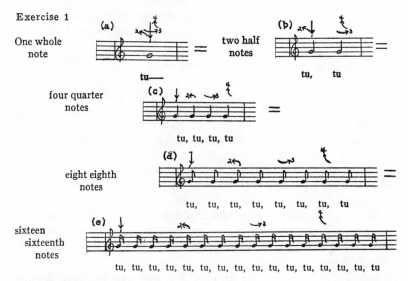

One whole note (a) = two half notes (b)

tu— tu, tu

four quarter notes (c) =

tu, tu, tu, tu

eight eighth notes (d) =

tu, tu, tu, tu, tu, tu, tu, tu

sixteen sixteenth notes (e)

tu, tu, tu, tu, tu, tu, tu, tu, tu, tu, tu, tu, tu, tu, tu, tu

These five measures should be drilled over and over until the physiological rhythm of the conductor's beat and the spoken syllables have become the signs in the mind of the student. There is no escape from this fundamental drill for if it is not done and done thoroughly, it may be years before the reversed mental act will become automatic, which is, that the signs call forth the rhythmic pattern.

Of course, these signs are called *notes* and are known as whole notes, half notes, quarter notes, eighth notes, and sixteenth notes. Thirty-second notes and sixty-fourth notes are not included in EMERGENT VOICE for they are seldom used in vocal music, being too fast for vocal performance unless the music is extremely slow, and in vocal music slow rhythms are generally represented by halves and quarter notes as in hymns.

FOUR PULSE RHYTHM

The rhythmic patterns which follow are the most usual single measure rhythms in ⁴⁄₄ time, using half and quarter notes. They should be practiced with the same method and diligence as Exercise 1.

Exercise 2

Through all of these early simple rhythmic figures, the teacher should illustrate the body rhythm with the accompanied spoken syllables, before allowing the student to look at the measure representing that rhythm. This should be repeated until the sight of the measure calls for the conductor's beat and the syllables which that measure represents. In other words, Exercise 2

Exercise 3

Exercise 4

should not be an attempt to beat the two half notes, but the teacher himself should give the

conductor's beat  with its ac-

companying *tu-u, tu-u,* have the student practice it and *then* look at the two half notes which represent it. For many centuries people sang, swaying their bodies, clapping their hands and tapping their feet before man conceived the idea of representing these rhythms with signs. It took many more centuries to evolve those signs into our present note system. Today practically all music teachers expect their pupils to start with the sign and work back to the rhythm instead of starting with the rhythm and working toward the sign.

When these single-measure rhythmic figures have become automatic they should be put together in two- and four-measure phrases, using all kinds of combinations for experience in reading varied rhythmic patterns with ease.

Exercise 5

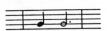

Exercise 6

In Exercise 5 a new sign appears: the use of the dot. The dot always represents half the value of the rhythmic pulse of the note which it follows. That means that the dot following the half note of Exercise 5 makes that dotted

Exercise 7

half note ($\downarrow$.) represent the  of the

four beats of common march time instead of its

regular  . In the study of rhythms in the

human body, arm and hand movements are primary, leg and feet movements secondary. Even in the embryo the hands start to develop before the feet, and after birth, a baby will keep time to a band with his arms and hands even before he can walk. For this reason, the conductor's beat is more fundamental in rhythmic patterning than foot tapping or marching, for it gives the basic arm and hand movements in the rhythmic patterns which the vocalist must follow all his life under either choral or orchestral leadership.

Now that we have practiced the simple heart beat rhythm, the next natural step is to become acquainted with the normal patterns emerging from the simplest division of that beat. The following are the most usual patterns in that first division, and are made up of quarter and eighth notes.

The rhythmic pattern of Exercise 1-c is our fundamental rhythm and Exercise 8 shows the sign for the 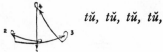 *tŭ, tŭ, tŭ, tŭ,*

thump-thump, thump-thump, of four regular heart beats, used on a
single breath pulse in youth. The process of teaching should still be
from rhythmic pulse to sign.

Exercise 8   Exercise 9   Exercise 10   Exercise 11

Exercise 12   Exercise 13   Exercise 14   Exercise 15

Exercise 16   Exercise 17   Exercise 18   Exercise 19

Exercise 20

One of the most usual patterns in this second division of the heart
beat is the pulse and a half followed by the half pulse, represented by
the dotted quarter and eighth. In the simplest form, Exercise 21, we
have the signs representing the carry-over of the first pulse into the
second with the last half of the second spoken by itself, being exactly
the same as Exercise 9 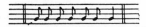 *tŭ, tŭ-tŭ, tŭ, tŭ,* ex-
                                           1   2   3   4

cept that it represents the first half of the second pulse tied to the first

as [music] but now written [music] and representing

the spoken *tŭ-ŭ, tŭ, tŭ, tŭ.* The teacher should illustrate the con-
          1 2   3   4
ductor's beat and spoken *tŭ, tŭ-tŭ, tŭ, tŭ* of Exercise 9 and the con-
                          1   2   3   4
ductor's beat and spoken *tŭ-ŭ, tŭ, tŭ, tŭ* of Exercise 21 and the tied
                          1 2   3   4
form and dotted quarter form shown above, which show the change
caused by the carry-over.

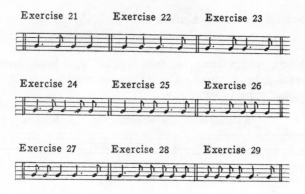

After these twenty-nine exercises have been drilled from body rhythms into the signs until the sight of any measure calls for the corresponding body rhythm, then two- and four-measure rhythmic patterns of all types of combinations of these measures should be written out and drilled.

A search through a standard hymn book or folk song book, looking for one-, two-, and four-measure rhythmic patterns like the ones already drilled, will immediately show the need for the study of the signs used in music to represent *rests*. From the beginning of his musical experience, the student of music should realize that a rest in music is actually a place where the rhythmic pulse continues but the performer doesn't sing.

RESTS

The rests in music naturally follow the same rhythmic patterns as the singing, for they too come from normal body rhythms. We sing with these rhythms and we rest with these rhythms.

The sign which has been developed to represent a *whole* measure of rest, whatever the time, is called a whole rest and is a solid black

Ex. 30

bar, suspended from the fourth line of the staff. ≣━━≣ In com-

mon time (⁴⁄₄—march time), it represents a rest of the whole rhythmic

figure ♩♩♩♩ being equal to the time of the whole note. ≣━o━≣

The following exercises will show the signs for the rests in relationship to the notes which they represent.

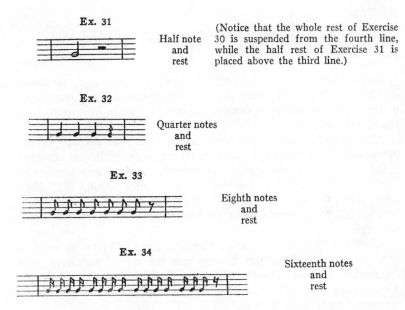

Ex. 31

Half note
and
rest

(Notice that the whole rest of Exercise 30 is suspended from the fourth line, while the half rest of Exercise 31 is placed above the third line.)

Ex. 32

Quarter notes
and
rest

Ex. 33

Eighth notes
and
rest

Ex. 34

Sixteenth notes
and
rest

The thirty-second note and rest ♪, and the sixty-fourth note and rest ♪, are not usual in vocal music. The reason is simple. Unless the music is slow in rhythm, they are too fast to be sung, except as embellishments. Let the student take a regular march time rhythm, saying *tŭ, tŭ, tŭ, tŭ* for the quarter notes. Then let him keep the same rhythm, doing *tŭtŭ, tŭtŭ, tŭtŭ, tŭtŭ,* for eighth notes. Now try *tŭtŭtŭtŭ, tŭtŭtŭtŭ, tŭtŭtŭtŭ, tŭtŭtŭtŭ,* for sixteenth notes. When he tries 8 thirty-second notes to a beat he will find that he cannot articulate that fast. If he changes the *tŭ* to *pŭtŭ,* he can almost perform it. He will find that no trick of articulation can bring his speed up to sixteen sixty-fourth notes to a beat. For this reason vocal music is mostly written and sung with ♩, ♩, ♩, ♪, ♪, notes.

Now let the student practice all the rhythmic figures from Exercise 2 to Exercise 29, using rests at different beats in the rhythmic measure, until all the signs for rests become as automatic as the signs for notes.

Ex. 35   Ex. 36

Exercise 2, for instance, can be done two ways:

Exercise 3, as simple as it is, will suffice to show how varied the rhythmic patterns may become when rests are used:

Ex. 37

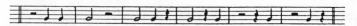

When rests come into use, rhythmic patterns become so numerous
that the fascination of body rhythms into signs and the recognition
of the signs into body rhythms is a game of intense interest to both
teacher and student.

The preceding analysis of the use of rests was necessary, even
before examining the simple patterns arising from eighth and sixteenth
notes, to facilitate the application work in reading and performing
rhythmic patterns. There are very few songs, like "Abide With Me,"
where the rhythmic patterns remain in the simple forms of whole notes,
half notes, and quarter notes without rests or variations from simple
rhythmic patterns.

To finish our presentation of Common Time (4/4) let us examine
some of the simple patterns arising from the use of eighth (♪) and
sixteenth (♬) notes. The straight sixteenth form is found in Exercise
1-e on page 101. The following are some of the more simple and
common forms:

Of course one recognizes instantly that the smaller the divisions,
the more numerous the combinations. For instance, the above figure
mixed with its reverse form might give us:

Ex. 41

One of the most usual single pulse rhythmic figures in vocal music
using eighth and sixteenth notes is where the eighth and first sixteenth
of the rhythmic figure ♪♬ are tied together ♪♬ and written   ♪.♪

The following rhythmic pattern from "The Battle Cry of Freedom" will serve to illustrate its familiar use:

Ex. 42

Shouting   the   battle   cry   of   freedom

or the beginning of "Love's Old Sweet Song:"

Ex. 43

Once   in the dear dead   days beyond   recall

The rhythmic pattern of the dotted eighth and sixteenth (the second pulse of both the above exercises) originates from the *word emphasis in poems*. Any two syllables with emphasis on the first, is spoken or sung in this rhythmic pattern.

The writer has made all the rhythmic figures on single pitches, so that the eye in its early training can more quickly grasp the sign forms.

TWO PULSE RHYTHM

Two-four time is not ⁴⁄₄ halved, but is the most basic rhythm of all. It represents the *thump-thump* of the two heart beats occurring on each inspiration and expiration in early youth. [See page 99.] All of its regular rhythmic figures can be found, however, in the exercises on ⁴⁄₄ time. Its sign in the conductor's beat is *down, up:*

Several typical measures follow. They should be easy for the student to read for they are even more basic than the ⁴⁄₄ measures already studied.

Ex. 44

TRIPLETS AND 6/8 TIME

When one divides a single rhythmic pulse into three small energy surges, the three pulse surge is called a triplet. In ²⁄₄ time it is designated by writing three eighth notes with a small figure 3 above or below to show that three eighths are to be performed in the time of two:

Ex. 45

tu,   tu-tu,   tu,   tu-tu-tu,   tu,   tu-tu,   etc.
1   2———   1   2———

This form of rhythmic pulse is quickly recognized if one will say the words out loud to the old round: "Row, row, row your boat gently down the stream; *Merrily, merrily, merrily, merrily,* life is but a dream."

In rhythmic pattern it would look like this:

Ex. 46

Row, row, row your boat gently down the stream;

Merrily, merrily, merrily, merrily, life is but a dream.

When triplets are used on each beat of two pulse rhythm through-out a song, as in:

Ex. 47

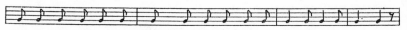

Little Tom Tinker got burned with a clinker and he began to cry___,

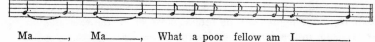

Ma_____, Ma_____, What a poor fellow am I_____.

then we give it a new name and call it ⅝ time, substituting for the triplet sign, the dotted quarter note which divides equally into three eighth notes. It is still the basic rhythm of two heart beats, but now each pulse is divided into three small pulses, making six eighth notes to the measure. The dotted quarter note (♩.) now represents the heart beat instead of the quarter note (♩) as in ²⁄₄ time.

Practice the following typical measures, first speaking them with *tŭ*'s and then reading the signs, until the rhythmic patterns are easily recognized.

Ex. 48

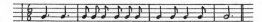

In ⅝ time, the same conductor's beat is used as in ²⁄₄ time—the regular *down-up* beat—the performer feeling the three pulse rhythm on each beat. Starting with such simple things as some of the children's favorites, *Hey, Diddle, Diddle* and *Dickory, Dickory, Dock,* and proceeding to old familiar songs, as *It Came Upon a Midnight Clear, Silent Night,* and the chorus of *Sailing, Sailing,* study the 6/8 rhythms by the spoken method into sight. Six-eight time will be found to be not only simple, but all its rhythmic figures delightfully easy. All kinds of combinations should be practiced, always from the rhythm to the sign, until the sign to the rhythm becomes automatic.

If the student has studied carefully the paragraph about the changing relationship of heart beat and breath pulse (page 99), noting the progressive emergence from three beats to four as the child grows to adult life, he has probably asked this question: "Why, if 3/4 time is more primitive than 4/4, has the author given all the basic rhythms of 4/4, 2/4, and 6/8 times before he has started the patterns of 3/4 time?"

The reason 4/4 time has been placed first in EMERGENT VOICE is that the largest percentage of people who will study EMERGENT VOICE will be those to whom 4/4 time is now the basic rhythm—those in late youth and early adult life. The 6/8 and 2/4 rhythms are most fascinating to childhood because of the very rapid heart beat of little children. A most interesting study in rhythm is the perusal of the rhythmic patterns of some popular book of children's songs. The song book for children which has probably been the most popular of all the Mother Goose books during the last quarter of a century, has only three songs in 4/4 time. Thirty-five of its songs are in 6/8 and 2/4 time. The author's two daughters, when they were little tots, did not like those three songs in 4/4 time until they were taught to sing them in 2/4 time. There was one song in the book written in 6/4 time but it was actually in 6/8 time and every child sings it with the rollicking freedom of a regular 6/8 rhythm. This recognition of the 2/4 *thump-thump* of the heart beat used on inspiration and expiration as a basic rhythmic measure and the two pulse rhythm of 6/8 time is normal in all small children.

6/4 TIME

Six-four time, like 6/8, is a two pulse rhythm, but the time unit is now a dotted half note (𝅗𝅥.) instead of a dotted quarter (♩.). The following are simple, typical measures:

Ex. 49

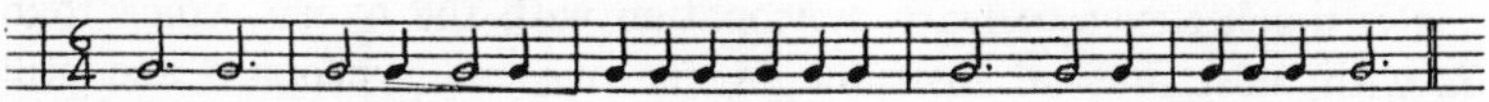

THREE PULSE RHYTHMS

The conductor's beat for a three pulse rhythmic pattern is pictured

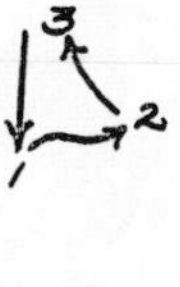

and is taught *down, out, up,* for its 1, 2,3 beat. When the

conducting pattern is learned and the following typical figures practiced, it will be found to be easy to the student, for it is more primitive
than $\frac{4}{4}$, in its quarter note form, which is called Waltz Time ($\frac{3}{4}$).

Ex. 50

9/8 TIME

When the unit of time is a dotted quarter note instead of the
quarter, then the time signature becomes $\frac{9}{8}$ and each rhythmic unit is
divided into three notes instead of two. The following measures are
typical of $\frac{9}{8}$ time but the conductor's beat is still the same as in $\frac{3}{4}$.

Ex. 51

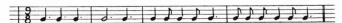

Four measure figures of all types should be built from the above
and practiced both in $\frac{3}{4}$ and $\frac{9}{8}$ time.

EMERGENT VOICE is not a music theory book. It has included
enough rhythmic theory to give the vocal student a foundation in
musicianship and to "whet his appetite" for knowledge in a field in
which he must excel if he is to thoroughly enjoy his singing.

SYNCOPATION

We cannot leave the rhythmic patterns without at least a glimpse
at syncopation. There seems to be a natural thrill in getting ahead
of the regular beat in music rhythms. This winning out by rushing the
pulse, "beating the beat" by throwing it forward to the unaccented
pulse of the rhythm is called syncopation. It is a very simple and usual
variation from regular rhythmic figures. Everybody likes it. It is almost
druglike in its ability to "put a kick" in the common rhythmic pulse.

The simplest form, of course, is that shown in Exercise 7 on page
102, where the secondary accent normally coming on the third beat in
common time (♩ ♩ ♩ ♩) is moved forward to the second beat (♩ ♩ ♩).

It is much easier to learn syncopation with the human voice than
it is with most musical instruments, for one can syncopate and still
retain the regular rhythmic pulse with an energy surge on the regular
accent.

The following exercise should be thoroughly drilled:

Ex. 52

After the above simple forms are mastered, the student may study the following exercises which show the necessity of acquiring a thorough knowledge of rhythmic patterns for the reading of song literature.

Exercise 53 is from Mozart's "Alleluja," [3] while Exercise 54 is from MacFayden's "Love Is the Wind." [4] These syncopations are typical of the rhythmic problems confronting any student as he builds his repertoire.

Ex. 53

Except for the syncopations, these two exercises are made up entirely of figures already practiced and should not be difficult to master.

Ex. 54

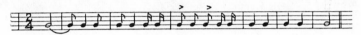

[3] W. A. Mozart, *Alleluja*. New York: G. Schirmer, Inc., 1929.
[4] Alexander MacFayden, *Love Is the Wind*. New York: John Church·Co., 1911.

CHAPTER XI

THEORY: MELODIC AND HARMONIC READING

I T IS the writer's firm belief that anyone who has normal hearing and a normal throat can learn to sing beautifully and read music accurately. For melodic and harmonic reading, *normal hearing* is as essential to the student as are his heart beat, nerve pulses, and breath pulse for rhythmic reading. Without normal hearing and a normal throat, it is impossible for the student to build melodic and harmonic reading patterns, for he cannot match vibration rates. Just as rhythmic reading should be studied from doing the rhythms first and then learning the signs that are used to represent them, so melodic and harmonic practice should be hearing and singing first, and then studying the signs for the music heard and sung.

All sound is based on the ability of the human ear to detect differences in vibration rates. As we saw in Chapters IV and V, these rates may be the pitches we are singing or playing, or by combinations of rates they may create a quality to the sound in singing which we designate as a vowel, or in the case of musical instruments these combinations of fundamental and overtones are called the *quality* or *timbre* of the instrument.

Almost all tones, when produced, have not only the fundamental rate of the pitch involved, such as an a' with its 440 vibrations per second, but also have a series of *overtones* or *upper partials* which vibrate with them. These faster vibrations are always in mathematical relation to the fundamental tone. For instance, if we start with the lowest tone on the piano keyboard, we find that it is called a *subcontra a* and is written AAA and has $27\frac{1}{2}$ vibrations per second. The next octave higher is called *contra a,* is written AA and has two times as many vibrations per second (55). The next octave a is called a *great a,* is written A and has four times the vibrations of AAA ($27\frac{1}{2}$) or 110 vibrations per second, the next octave eight times, etc. The series of pitches from the lowest a on the keyboard to the a three tones from the top of the keyboard would be AAA-$27\frac{1}{2}$, AA-55, A-110, a-220, a'-440 (this is the a above middle c), a''-880, a'''-1760, and a''''-3520. Of course one sees instantly that these are in the mathematical proportion of 1, 2, 4, 8, 16, 32, 64, 128 times the original AAA ($27\frac{1}{2}$).

OVERTONES

We might call these the octave overtones, but they do not constitute the full overtone series. The full *overtone* or *upper partial* series is in the mathematical relationship of 1, 2, 3, 4, 5, 6, 7, 8, 9, 10, 11, 12, 13, 14, 15, 16, etc. Most people give no attention to their latent ability to recognize the relative strength of these overtones. Some of our greatest orchestral conductors have such keen perception of the relative strength of power of the first eight overtones that they can actually tell the relative strength of the blending of the overtones that are responsible for the quality of tone of the clarinet, trumpet, French horn, etc. Modern sound machinery recordings have proven this ability to be accurate. One of the main reasons for the writer's intense interest in research was that his keenness of hearing made him painfully aware of the "out-of-tuneness" of varying vowel colors within the sections of practically all choral groups. There are almost no choral groups in America whose vowel pitches are blended within the sections, especially on the English lax vowels ĭ (as in *sit*), ĕ (as in *them*), ŏŏ (as in *look*), ŭ (as in *dust*). There are very few choral conductors with the keenness of perception of F. Melius Christiansen and his son Olaf, both of whom, by their quick recognition and blending of vibrato, pitch, and vowel beats, have made St. Olaf's Choir of Northfield, Minnesota, so well-known.

EMERGENT VOICE is only interested in the most basic melodic and harmonic forms, the forms which arise from the first six sounds of the overtone series. The normal hearing of any individual gives him the equipment for recognition of those tones and their relationships. The voice student who wishes to study theoretical music should go beyond the things presented in this text to regular work in that field.

If we start with C below middle C and write out the scale letter names of the first six of the overtone series, we would have *c*, *c′*, *g′*, *c′′*, *e′′*, *g′′*. If we use our octave knowledge which we have already discovered through our study of the A pitches on the keyboard, and bring all of these tones into the octave between middle C (*c′*) and the next octave above (*c′′*) we would have *c′*, *e′*, *g′*, *c′′*. These pitches constitute what is called the *tonic chord*. This means it is the basic overtone series from a fundamental tone (in this case *c*) all placed within one octave.

The following figure shows the keys of the piano keyboard from *c′* to *c′′* with letters, figures, and the tonic chord indicated.

Ex. 55

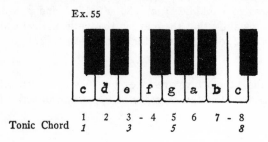

Tonic Chord   1 2 3 - 4 5 6 7 - 8
              1   3   5   8

Notice that there are eight tones represented by the white keys in the octave from *c'* to *c''*. It now becomes necessary to throw away the mathematical figures of the overtone series in our musical thinking and use those adopted by music. The eight tones of the white keys from *c'* to *c''* are called a major diatonic scale and are numbered from 1 to 8, so the C scale with its letters *c, d, e, f, g, a, b, c* are numbered 1, 2, 3, 4, 5, 6, 7, 8 and the tonic chord is called a 1, 3, 5, 8 chord. The first three tones of this tonic chord (1, 3, 5) are called the tonic triad. This triad, because it contains the fundamental outline of the first six overtones, is basic in both melodic and harmonic reading.

Look carefully at Exercise 55 and note the difference in the number of tones between 1 and 3 and the number between 3 and 5. One will see instantly that there are four semitones between 1 and 3 but only three semitones between 3 and 5. Intervals in music, the distance between one tone and another in the diatonic scale, are counted from the lower tone to the upper, calling the lower tone 1. Thus in the 1-3-5 of the tonic triad there are two thirds. The interval from 1 to 3 and the interval from 3 to 5 are both thirds. The third from 1 to 3 with its four semitones is called a *major third,* while the interval from 3 to 5 is called a *minor third* (it is minus one semitone). The major third being on the bottom of the tonic triad of *c-e-g* (1-3-5) this triad is called a *major triad.* This is its natural position in the overtone series and satisfies the normal hearing as being fundamental. If the 3 of the 1-3-5 were lowered one half step and the triad was *c-eb-g* instead of *c-e-g* (the flat sign—b—is used to lower a tone one half step), then the prominence of the minor third on the bottom of the triad would create a depressed feeling in our hearing processes and we would call it a *minor triad.* There are two related minor triads to every major triad. The one described above is called the *tonic minor,* meaning that it is built from the same tone, and the other the *relative minor.* The relative minor to the *c-e-g* major triad leaves the major third of the *c-e* intact and instead of using the *e-g* above adds the *a-c* minor third below. This *a-c-e* minor triad is so closely *related* to the major *c-e-g* triad that it is called the *relative minor* to the *c-e-g* major triad. These major and minor triads are basic in the musical equipment of any voice student, for in the 1-2-3∪4-5-6-7∪8 of the major scale with its half steps between 3 and 4, and 7 and 8 (see Exercise 55), 1-3-5 is major, 2-4-6 is minor, 3-5-7 is minor, 4-6-8 is major, 5-7-2 is major, 6-8-3 is minor, while 7-2-4 is a "double minor triad"—musicians call it a *diminished triad* for it is even diminished by one semitone from the regular minor triad.

Ex. 56   TRIADS BUILT ON THE MAJOR SCALE

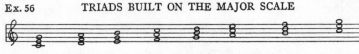

I	ii	iii	IV	V	vi	vii°	I
Major	Minor	Minor	Major	Major	Minor	Diminished	Major

Just as the triad 7-2-4 is a double minor, if one takes the 1-3-5 and
sharps the 5 as in *c-e-g♯* (the sharp sign—♯—is used to raise a tone
one half step), he obtains a "double major triad"—musicians call
this an *augmented triad* for it is augmented by an extra half step
beyond the regular major triad. [See Exercise 9 of Series III, page
94.] These double minors and double majors have vast importance
in modern music and make the old system of sight-reading by *do, re,
mi*'s practically worthless, except for melodies in simple major and
minor scales.

The first basic ability in melodic and harmonic reading, for the
vocalist, is the complete, thorough, and perfect mastery of the major
and minor triad. This mastery must be threefold: hearing, singing, and
seeing.

Starting with the major triad, which is the natural position of the
sounds in the regular overtone series, let the student hear the sound
of the triad *c-e-g* (1-3-5) played melodically, that is, with the tones
in succession *c ⁄ e ⁄ g ＼ e ＼ c* (1 ⁄ 3 ⁄ 5 ＼ 3 ＼ 1). After the melodic form
is familiar in hearing, let him hum it while he listens to the triad again
and again.

Now, either with a light hum or with some easy neutral syllable
like *lä*, practice the triad in every conceivable form, 1 ⁄ 3 ⁄ 5 ＼ 3 ＼ 1,
5 ＼ 3 ＼ 1 ⁄ 3 ⁄ 5, 1 ⁄ 5 ＼ 3, 5 ＼ 1 ⁄ 3, 3 ＼ 1 ⁄ 5, 3 ⁄ 5 ＼ 1, 1 ⁄ 3 ＼ 1 ⁄ 5,
5 ＼ 3 ⁄ 5 ＼ 1, 3 ＼ 1 ⁄ 5 ＼ 3, 3 ⁄ 5 ＼ 1 ⁄ 3, 3 ⁄ 3 ＼ 5 ⁄ 5 ＼ 1 ＼ 3 ⁄ 5,
1 ＼ 1 ⁄ 3 ⁄ 3 ＼ 5 ＼ 3 ＼ 1, etc. Whether in class work or privately, do not
leave the major triad until it is completely, thoroughly, and perfectly
mastered. Now it is time for the student to *see* the major triad as it
appears in written music.

Through the hundreds of years that music signs have been developed, there have been numerous attempts to build a simple system by
which the musician can quickly *see* pitches. The final outcome of these
attempts is an eleven lined staff, five lines above, five lines below, with
a central short line between (the Great Staff). This central short line
is called *Middle C* (*c'*), and is truly middle C for it is the middle of
the singing range of all human voices combined. It is near the top of
the ordinary man's voice and near the bottom of the ordinary woman's
voice; in fact it can be sung by men, women, and children, old and
young, high and low voices.

Ex. 57

GREAT
STAFF

The two signs, $\oint$ and $\mathcal{9}$: are called clefs. The $\oint$ clef (G-clef), also called the treble clef, fixes the pitch of g' on the second line of the upper staff. The $\mathcal{9}$: clef (F-clef), also called the bass clef, fixes the pitch of f on the fourth line of the lower staff. It will be noticed immediately that the upper staff, with its octave, c' to c'', carries the pitches sung by women's voices and unchanged boys' voices, while the lower staff, with its octave, c to c', carries the pitches sung by men's voices.

If the three major triads, referred to on page 116 were placed on this staff they would look like this:

Ex. 58

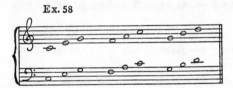

In numbers they are 1-3-5, 4-6-8, and 5-7-2 both on the treble and bass clefs. In letters they are c-e-g, f-a-c, and g-b-d both on the treble and bass clefs. If a man were reading them on the treble clef, he would naturally sing them an octave lower and would actually be singing them as they appear on the bass clef. If a woman were reading them on the bass clef, she would naturally *sing* them an octave higher as if they were written on the treble clef. Exercises should always be played in the octave in which the student sings—women's exercises in the treble clef and men's in the bass clef. Part of the growth of any student's basic musicianship should be the development of the ability to recognize instantly the octave in which any voice or instrument is singing or playing. Only for convenience' sake are the exercises of EMERGENT VOICE written in the treble clef. When played for men they should be played an octave lower than written so that the pitches are actually in a man's range. The author has known many voice students who have studied for years and never developed the fundamental recognition of the difference in the sound of tones in the treble and bass clefs.

Because the *letter names* of the figures 1, 2, 3, 4, 5, 6, 7, 8 of the diatonic scale change every time the key changes, these figures have been given names which describe their position in the scale. Numbers 1 and 8 are called the *Tonic* from the Latin word which means "tone,"

for they are the main tones of the scale, the 8 being twice as fast as
the 1 in vibration rates and actually being the 1 of the same scale an
octave higher. The fifth is called the *Dominant*, for next to 1 it domi-
nates the scale. Being the first overtone beyond the octave it is next
in importance to the octave in our hearing mechanism. Its interval of
the 5th above the tonic is also the basic interval for the building of new
scales, for transposition and for harmonic progressions. Number 4 is
called the *Subdominant* for it is the underdominant, being the fifth
below the octave. If we start from the Key of C, the dominant (a fifth
upward) starts the cycle of sharp keys while the subdominant (a fifth
downward) starts the cycle of flat keys. Number 3 is called the
Mediant for it is the middle tone of the tonic triad, 1-3-5 (the tonic-
mediant-dominant). Number 6 is called the *Submediant* for it is the
middle tone of the subdominant triad, 4-6-8 (subdominant-submediant-
tonic). Number 2 is called the *Supertonic* for it is *above* or *super* to
the tonic. Number 7 is called the *Leading Tone* for it is practically
impossible to sing it in any progression without feeling an urge to be
led into the tonic.

In their order they are: *1—Tonic, 2—Supertonic, 3—Mediant,
4—Subdominant, 5—Dominant, 6—Submediant, 7—Leading Tone,
8—Tonic.*

We call the triads and chords of *any key* by these names. Hence
the 1-3-5 of any key is called the Tonic Triad, the 5-7-2 is called the
Dominant Triad, and the 4-6-8 is the Subdominant Triad.

The student should now write exercises in both the treble and bass
clefs in the Key of C using the major triads with different time signatures and all the rhythmic figures of Chapter IX.

By this time, the drill in the major triad and rhythmic figures should
be so completely and thoroughly mastered that an exercise as simple
as the following, in either clef, can be read at sight without difficulty.

Ex. 59

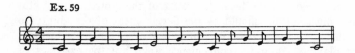

Naturally the above melody sounds like a bugle call, for the tones
of the bugle are the tones of the overtone series. [See page 113.]

The next step for the vocalist is the complete mastery of the minor
triad, both as a separate entity and in its relationship to the major triad.
Taking the major triad in its 1∕3∕5∖3∖1 form in the Key of C
(*c∕e∕g∖e∖c*), lower the *e* one half step to *eb* and play the triad
c∕eb∕g∖eb∖c, both melodically and harmonically.

Ex. 60

Now drill the minor triad in all possible forms as was done with the major triad on page 116. In relationship to the major triad, this minor triad is called the *tonic minor* for it is built from the same *tone* as the major triad. Practice it in all its forms in relationship to the major triad (as in Exercise 60).

After the major and minor triads are thoroughly mastered by hearing, singing, and seeing them, write them with different rhythmic figures to develop eye-sight patterns for their reading in both major and minor.

We should now drill the *relative minor* triad described on page 115, in relationship to the major triad. The relative minor is found by adding a minor third below the major tonic triad. In figures, it means that we add the 6 of the scale below the 1-3-5 and use the *6-1-3* for a triad. This relative minor triad represents the tonic triad of the nearest related minor key, for we do not have to change any pitches as we did in the tonic minor of the same key. In other words, in the Key of C, *c-eb-g* would be the *tonic minor* triad derived from C *major*, but the *relative minor* triad of *c-e-g* would be *a-c-e*, which is more closely related for it already exists in the C scale. It is the *tonic* triad of the key of A *minor*. [See Exercise 61.]

The piano keyboard starts with an A at the bottom and stops with a C at the top. Take the *c'* (middle C) and play the white notes from *c'* to *c''* and then play the *c'-e'-g'-c''* (1-3-5-8) of that scale and listen to the harmony. Now take the *a* below *c'* and play the *a-b-c'-d'-e'-f'-g'-a'* (all white keys), and play the 1-3-5-8 from the *a* (*a-c'-e'-a'*). Play, listen, sing, and write the two scales and chords.

Ex. 61
C major   A minor (relative minor of C major)

There are several forms of minor scales, but we will leave them for the study of musical theory of a more advanced nature than the simple fundamentals presented in EMERGENT VOICE.

THE MAJOR SCALE

By this time, every curious student is beginning to wonder how the major scale with its 1-2-3⌣4-5-6-7⌣8 gets its form. We will not go into its historical development. We will let the student build one. We have already seen that the 5th is the dominant because it is the first overtone beyond the octave. In the Key of C the first three tones of the overtone series are, of course, c'-c''-g''. Let us put the g down an octave and we get c'-g'-c''. Now find the dominant of g. We start with the g overtone series, which is always the octave and then the 5th above —it is g'-g''-d''. So the d, a 5th above the g, is the dominant of g. If we bring it down into our octave, we now have c'-d'-g'-c''. Continuing the same way, we find that a is the dominant of d, that e is the dominant of a, that b is the dominant of e. If these are all placed in one octave we would have the scale c-d-e-   -g-a-b-c. Only the f is missing. Every interval which added a new tone in the above scale formation was a perfect fifth above the last tone until we get to this missing f. This time the perfect fifth above the b would be an $f\sharp$ but the human race has decided on f for the final tone of the so-called major scale. To the author this is perfectly natural for the $f\natural$ is the subdominant of the original c' from which we started the scale and is a perfect fifth below our tonic. The human ear seems to prefer this f which lies only a perfect 5th below our basic tone, rather than the $f\sharp$ which lies six perfect 5ths above.

We now find that our natural major scale, built by perfect fifths from our original c', when condensed into a single octave becomes c'-d'-$e'\smile f'$-g'-a'-$b'\smile c''$. This scale is built up completely by the use of the octave and the perfect fifth (the first two overtones of the natural laws of sound) condensed by the use of the octave interval, into the single octave range of c' to c''.

When we number it 1-2-3$\smile$4-5-6-7$\smile$8 and look at its construction on the piano, as in Exercise 55, page 114, we see that between 3 and 4 (e' and f') and between 7 and 8 (b' and c'') there are no black keys. These two intervals in the scale are only half as large as all the others and are called *half steps* or *semitones*. The distance between 1 and 2 (c' and d') and all the other steps in the scale with a black key between, are called *whole tones* or *whole steps*.

INTERVALS

The distance between one pitch and another is called an interval. Distances between two tones are figured from the lower tone to the upper tone by numbers. In the scale we can count intervals from any tone to another.

Exercise 62

(1)   c-d-e$\smile$f-g-a-b$\smile$c
(2)   1-2-3$\smile$4-5-6-7$\smile$8
(3)   1-2$\smile$3-4-5-6$\smile$7
(4)   1$\smile$2-3-4-5$\smile$6

Two or more tones of the same pitch sung together, are called a unison. When figuring intervals in music, the lower tone must always be figured as 1.

Scale numbers start from the tonic. *Interval* numbers can start from any tone in any key. Thus the scale numbers and intervals will be the same from the tonic but not from any other tone of the scale.

The interval name from 1 to 2 is a *second,* from 1 to 3 is a *third,* from 1 to 4 is a *fourth,* from 1 to 5 a *fifth,* from 1 to 6 a *sixth,* from 1 to 7 a *seventh,* and from 1 to 8 an *octave,* going on with the 9th, 10th, 11th, etc.

When a second consists of a whole step, it is called a *major second,* as c to d of Exercise 62-(2). If it is only a half step as in Exercise 62-(4) between e and f, it is called a *minor second.*

So the interval c to e of Exercise 62-(2)—1 to 3—is a *major third,* while the interval from d to f, Exercise 62-(3)—1 to 3—is a *minor third,* being made up of a major second and a minor second instead of two major seconds as in the c to e.

The following chart will give the student the regular complete interval picture in the Key of C from the tonic to the other tones of the major scale.

Ex. 63

| Perfect Unison | Major 2nd | Major 3rd | Perfect 4th | Perfect 5th | Major 6th | Major 7th | Perfect Octave |

When the major interval becomes smaller by a half step, through flatting the upper tone or sharping the lower tone, it is called a minor interval. Thus c to e is a major third but c to eb or c♯ to e is a minor third.

When the perfect fourth or fifth are made a half step smaller by flatting the upper tone or sharping the lower tone, they are called diminished. Thus c to g is a perfect fifth but c to gb or c♯ to g are diminished fifths.

When a minor interval is made a half step larger by the upper tone being sharped or the lower tone being flatted, the minor becomes a major. Thus the minor third of d to f of Exercise 62-(3)—1 to 3— would be a major third if the f were sharped and the interval were d to f♯, or if the d were flatted and the interval were db to f. When a perfect interval or a major interval becomes larger by a half step through sharping the upper tone or flatting the lower tone, the interval is called an augmented interval. Thus c to g is a perfect fifth but c to g♯ or cb to g are augmented fifths.

By studying Exercises 62 and 63, the student will discover that when intervals are inverted—that is, when the lower tone is raised an octave or the upper tone is lowered an octave—majors become minor, and minors become major, but perfects remain perfect. Thus c to e, Exercise 62-(1)—1 to 3—is a major third but e to c, Exercise 62-(4) —1 to 6—is a minor sixth for it includes both the half steps of $e \smile f$ and $b \smile c$.

If the student of voice is to become proficient in sight-reading, he must know his intervals. The feel of the major and minor second, the major and minor third, the perfect fourth and fifth, the major and minor sixth, the major and minor seventh and the octave must be as sure to him as the fact that two and two make four. Interval reading in music must become as automatic as his eyesight in reading this sentence.

Through the exercises of Series II the student has already sung the five-tone diatonic scale, the major triad with its major and minor thirds, the perfect fourth with the *lä, mī, nō, gô* syllables of Exercise 5 (moving from d to g), the tonic, subdominant and dominant seventh chord lines in Exercise 6, and the octave in Exercise 8.

Now starting with the diatonic major scale of Exercise 61, page 119, he should start with c' and on some neutral syllable like *lä*, drill each interval from c' *to* c'' and from c'' to c'. Play $c' \diagup d' \diagdown c'$ on the piano, then sing *la, la, la* to the c', d', c' pitches until the major second can be sung from any tone. Now play $c' \diagup d' \diagup e' \diagdown c' \diagup e' \diagdown c'$ and sing *la, la, la, la, la, la* on those tones until a major third is a definite unit in hearing, singing, and sight.

When the major second and third are completely mastered, start at the top of the scale and with $c'' \diagdown b' \diagup c''$ (*la, la, la*) and $c'' \diagdown b' \diagdown a' \diagup$ $c'' \diagdown a' \diagup c''$ (*la, la, la, la, la, la*) drill the minor second and minor third until they become as thoroughly fixed as the major intervals. Continue this drill through all intervals within the octave, both from above and below. Write out exercises in rhythmic figures using the intervals and drill them with varying rhythmic patterns.

There is no short cut to musicianship, and this interval practice is as essential to the vocalist as technical exercises are to the pianist.

KEYS

The shifting of the major or minor scale, up or down to new levels of pitch, is necessary if different types of voices or instruments are able to sing or play melodies as they are written. So far only the key of C major and the relative A minor key have been explained. There are, in reality, as many keys as there are half steps between one octave and the next, either up or down. Just as our scale was built by fifths upward, so our sharp keys are built by a cycle of fifths upward.

The key of C major uses only white keys on the piano and consequently has no signature on the staff. [See Exercise 55, page 114, then Exercise 61, page 119.] If we move up five tones and start a scale from g', keeping the same relationship of whole and half steps as in the 1-2-3⌣4-5-6-7⌣8 of the key of C, we find that we have to use an f♯ to make the half step come between 7 and 8. g a b⌣c d e⌣f g gives
                                                 1 2 3⌣4 5 6 7⌣8
us the half step between 6 and 7 instead of between 7 and 8, where it must be if the scale sounds as a major scale. If we sharp the f and the scale is sung or played g a b⌣c d e f♯⌣g it becomes the
                                   1 2 3⌣4 5 6 7 ⌣8
diatonic major scale. In other words, the scale a perfect fifth above c' is a scale with *one sharp* and has its tonic on g', and the sharp added is the *leading tone*.

If we go on building our sharp keys, we will take the same cycle we did in our original scale building, the next sharp key being D with two sharps, then A with three sharps, then E with four sharps, B with five sharps, F♯ with six sharps, and C♯ with seven sharps.

If we start from c by perfect fifths downward, we find the first perfect fifth is the f (which we used in the diatonic scale). We now find that the scale from f must use the b♭ (subdominant of f) to sound like a major scale. This is self-evident' by numbering the f scale f g a b⌣c d e⌣f then lowering the pitch of the subdominant to make
1 2 3⌣4 5 6 7⌣8
the half step occur at the right place in the scale: f g a⌣bb♭ c d e⌣f
                                                  1 2 3⌣4 5 6 7⌣8
By the same cycle of fifths, except that this time they are by fifths downward, the flat keys are found: F, one flat; B♭, two flats; E♭, three flats; A♭, four flats; D♭, five flats; G♭, six flats; C♭, seven flats.

The following chart will show the major keys and their signatures:

Ex. 64

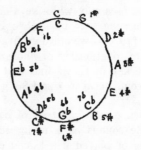

There are certain self-evident helps for quick recognition of key location on the staff which should be brought to the student's attention.

No signature on the staff indicates the key of C, for it uses no sharps or flats.

In sharp keys, the last sharp added (the farthest from the clef sign) is always the 7th (the leading tone) of the new key.

In the flat keys, the last flat added is always the 4th (the subdominant) of the new key. When more than one flat is used, the next to the last flat is the key note.

Quick identification is embodied in *"sharps seven, flats four."*

HARMONY

When the tones of the major tonic triad are heard in succession, c ∕ e ∕ g ∖ e ∖ c (1 ∕ 3 ∕ 5 ∖ 3 ∖ 1) we call it a melody. If they are arranged in a certain order (5 ∖ 3 ∖ 1 ∕ 3 ∕ 5 ∕ 8 in ¾ time with the following rhythmic pattern ♪.♪ | ♩♩♩ | ♩ the listener would say instantly "Why, that's the 'Star Spangled Banner'." If the same three tones were played simultaneously the resulting sound is called *harmony.*

The music of the world has emerged in the order of rhythm, melody, harmony. The most primitive music is only concerned with rhythms; as it advances, melody is added. Harmony is a comparatively recent development. In its simplest forms, harmonic progressions need only three triads or chords: the tonic (135), the dominant (572), and the subdominant (468). The dominant is very often enriched by adding another 3rd (5724) and is then called the *dominant seventh,* the 4 being a 7th above the dominant (5).

If we made chords out of these, arranged within the octave, we would have *1358, 1468, 2457.* When we write the signs for them on the treble clef, they will look like this:

Ex. 65

    I   IV   v⁷   I

These are the basic chords from which the vocalist must build his harmonic sense. Like the basic things of rhythm and melody, they must be sung, heard, and seen until the reverse of seeing, hearing, and singing becomes automatic.

So that the student may acquire the feel for tonic and dominant harmonies and tonic and subdominant harmonies, both major and minor, the following simple progressions should be sung, heard, and seen until when seen they can be heard and sung with flawless perfection.

Ex. 66   C major

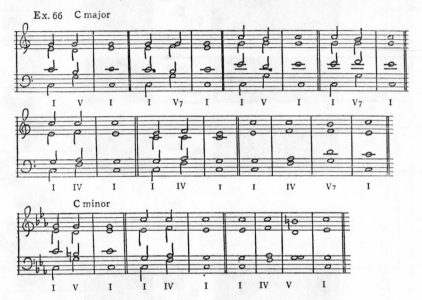

Although EMERGENT VOICE has no intention of being a theory text and is dealing only with the barest beginnings of rhythmic, melodic, and harmonic forms, we should include one exercise for the development of a seeing, hearing, and singing appreciation of the diminished and augmented chord forms found so frequently in modern music. The following simple exercise will meet that need.

Ex. 67

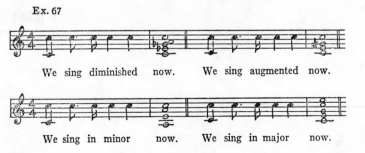

We sing diminished now.   We sing augmented now.

We sing in minor now.   We sing in major now.

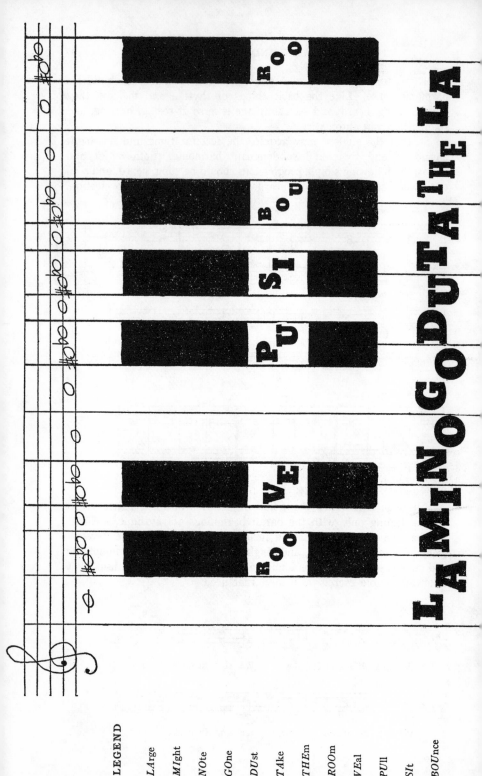

Chapter XII
LÄ-MĪ-NŌ-ZATION

THE greatest flaw in the development of musical notation has been that the system for sight-singing has not kept pace with the development of the notation for the writing and reading of instrumental music.

Since Guido D'Arrezo in the early 11th century noticed that the Hymn to St. John, written in 770, started its successive phrases with the syllables *ut, re, mi, fa, so, la* and that they made up the hexachord *c, d, e, f, g, a* we have spent 900 years changing the *ut* to *do*, adding the *si*, and changing the *si*, to *ti*. At that same time Guido invented the staff for recording music. During the same 900 years the signs used on that staff have travelled through hundreds of forms to arrive at the present efficient whole, half, quarter, eighth, sixteenth, thirty-second, and sixty-fourth notes, and their corresponding rests with simple key and time signatures.

Music itself, through that same 900 years has progressed through its many changes—Ecclesiastical, Classical, Romantic, Modern, Folk Song, Strophic, Ballade, Art Song to Oratorio, Opera, and Symphony—until modern music's undefined key relationships have made an *absolute* as well as a *relative* pitch sense essential to rapid sight-singing. The augmented and diminished intervals of modern harmonies and melodic forms have made *solmization* a hindrance instead of a help in the development of the musicianship of the vocalist. The lumbering, ox-cart inefficiency of *do-re-mi's* has become more and more evident as the automobile-airplane development of fast, syncopated rhythms, whole tone scales, diminished and augmented triads and chords have permanently found their places in musical compositions. The fifty-six names now used for the twelve semitones of the chromatic scale simply complicate, confuse, and hinder the musical development of the modern vocalist as he strives to become efficient as a sight-singing musician.

The basic idea of the *ut-re-mi* system was completely right, for the vocalist needs some syllabic sound as a sign to tie his tone to his hearing, eyesight, and muscle actions that he may pattern and condition those actions into simple, accurate, efficient, and automatic use. All of the attempts at improvement of the do-re-mi system have failed because of an innate original fault. There were not enough perfectly correlated, *singable* syllables, letters, or numbers to cover the chromatic scale in the *immovable dō* system and the *movable dō* failed to develop the musicianship of the vocalist in any way comparable to the musicianship of the instrumentalist who had to thoroughly master his techniques for each new key signature.

Lä-mĭ-nō-zation is the ultimate evolution of the original *ut-re-mi* thought. The syllables are perfect, phonetic correlations of English consonants and vowels. Physiologically they can be spoken or sung at the rate of ten to a second. In the laws of sound, not only the muscle actions but the vowel forms can be sung with perfect freedom in all keys (chromatically, diatonically, and rhythmically) at great speeds. The twelve syllables, using twelve different consonants correlated with twelve different vowel colors, as twelve immovable sounds on the twelve semitones of the chromatic scale make a simple and sure memory pattern in hearing, eyesight, and muscle action whose reflexes can be quickly patterned and conditioned to automatic use.

Vocally, when used with the principles of EMERGENT VOICE, the practice of sight-singing with *Lä-mĭ-nō-zation* develops beautiful, free, and resonant singing.

Because of the varying orchestral colors of the twelve sounds they are unbelievably efficient in the development of part-singing.

Because of the permanent location of the twelve dynamic syllables, the vocalist develops his musicianship in the manner of the instrumentalist, as he learns his scales and arpeggios in the keys of *lä*, *gô*, and *dŭ;* for he must add the flat or sharp of each new signature with its new syllable.

Because of the physiological speed and ease of articulation of these dynamic phonetics, they are flawless in any type of vocal sight-reading.

Because of the vowel arrangement in the chromatic and diatonic scales, they assist in voice development, for they fit the natural vowel-formant, overtone scale.

Because they use the signs already accepted in musical notation they do not interfere in any way with existing notation practice.

Because of their efficiency in application they can be used with any standard sight-singing book as a text.

The preceding chart is submitted as a practical, sure, quick, and efficient means for the development of a musicianly, sight-singing ability in the vocalist. If the preliminary work of Chapters IX and X has been thoroughly done, any standard sight-singing text such as "The Folk Song Sight Singing Series" Books I to X, by Crowe, Lawton and Whittaker (Oxford University Press—Carl Fischer) will make an excellent series for use of *Lä-mĭ-nō-zation* in the place of *do-re-mi*'s, for developing the sight-singing ability of the student into automatic, permanent use.

The use of *Lä-mī-nō-zation* will not only develop the relative pitch sense of the interval study of Chapter X but will ultimately develop in a great majority of vocal students the absolute pitch sense now only acquired through the long and careful study of some instrument like the violin or piano.

It is the author's firm belief that *Lä-mī-nō-zation* is the ultimate answer to all the controversies arising from attempts to build vocal musicianship through *solmization, tonic sol-fa, movable dō, immovable dō, interval reading, figure reading, letter reading,* "by guess and by gosh" reading, or what-have-you.

LÄ-MĪ-NŌ-ZATION is not just another attempt to solve a dis-agreeable problem. It is a scientific, physiological, phonetical, acousti-cal, and musical answer to a 900-year-old problem. Use it and it will prove its worth.

CHAPTER XIII

THE BOY'S VOICE

THE use of boy-choirs in the church service has naturally resulted in a literature on the development of the boy's voice. Practically all of this literature has been written on a false hypothesis—the hypothesis that a boy's voice is different from other voices and needs special treatment. All the silly "moo-mooing," "loo-looing" and "poo-pooing," resulting in the breathy, hooty, de-vitalized tone of most boys' choirs, should be "pooh-poohed" off the face of the earth and the boys given a chance to sing with the natural, clear, resonant, vital tone which is part and parcel of their normal physiological make-up.

Like any other human being, a boy can use clavicular, costal, or diaphragmatic (abdominal) breathing, he can produce tones that are clear or breathy, he can sing those tones fully resonated, with the balance of nasalization and oralization resulting from the greatest freedom in muscular controls, or he can block his nasal passages and get a nasal twang, block with his throat muscles and sound like he had a bag of mush in his throat, or blat those tones out of his mouth and scream on high pitches. Like any other human being he can articulate cleanly and distinctly or sloppily and lazily.

The author has personally developed every age of voice from kindergarten to octogenarian, every type of voice from *basso-profundo* to *coloratura*, every problem in voice from stuttering to the correction of the hollow voices of the totally deaf, and he would like to state with all the vehemence at his command that the principles and basic techniques for all voices of every type and age are identical—high and low, light and powerful, boys and girls, men and women, black, yellow, red, brown, and white, old and young. He has had the unusual experience of having whole kindergartens, in groups of fifty to a class, go into the first grade without a monotone left in the group. He has had the pleasure of having a grandmother sing again with the rich free tones of youth. He has had the keen enjoyment of introducing a deaf girl to a normal individual and have that deaf girl speak so normally and speech-read so rapidly that the normal individual was not aware of her deafness.

Whether it is the development of the normal singing or speaking voice, or the rehabilitation of subnormal or abnormal speaking or singing conditions, the framework of voice teaching techniques as given in EMERGENT VOICE is applicable to all cases except pathological or operative conditions. *The boy's voice is no exception.*

143

If a boy is to sing beautifully, he must use diaphragmatic breathing, with the abdominal lift for expiration controls; he must learn to sing with a clear tone; he must resonate his tones in every available cavity and bony structure of the head, with emphasis on freedom in nasalization; he must articulate with clean and precise accuracy. He has the same muscles and the same nerve controls as any other human being and demands the same positive techniques of development.

It is time the voice teaching profession recognized that *the correction of faults* is a waste of time and energy with any individual or group, and that voice teaching, like any athletic sport, should be taught positively, so that correct habits of voice emergence can displace faulty habits of blockings and interferences. Correct positive habits build a voice; and those correct positive habits are the basic techniques of diaphragmatic breathing, clear tones and freedom in nasalization from the *m*-hum. and clean and distinct articulation by vocalizing with English phonetic syllables. They emphasize the real task of the student as a producer—the task of learning how to handle his body for singing purposes. (A "trial and error" system of teaching voice is as ridiculous as it would be in golf, tennis or swimming.) Every fundamental detail of that task is the same for all voices—sopranos, altos, tenors, basses, little children, adults, boys, and girls. Matters of agility, range, power, and tone qualities are as individual as buck teeth, freckled faces, or bald heads; but the principles and the basic techniques for vocal development are the same for all.

The breathy tone illustrated in Plate III-D, or the hooty falsetto tone of Plate III-H, should not be tolerated in boys any more than they would be in an adult. As has been stated before, the falsetto tone has only one use—a usable production while developing the true mezza-voce. Many boy sopranos never develop a true, clear tone as in E, F, and G of Plate III, but always use the forms shown in Figures D and H. The author has known several young men in their twenties who had developed a breathy tone as boy sopranos, who carried this tone over into adult life and never learned to sing with the mechanism of their adult speaking voices—young men who would talk in a normal baritone speaking voice but when they sang, used the devitalized production of Figures D and H of Plate III.

It is the author's opinion that future research will ultimately show that the breathy tone of the middle range and the more refined breathy tone of the upper range (under the name of falsetto) are actually the same kind of production in all voices. Even in women's voices the same types exist, except that they are not so easily discernible because of the lack of the additional octave which men acquire during adolescence. The constant appearance of the problematic "two voiced" student, whether man, woman or child, always presents the same problem—

a breathy tone caused by inverted breathing and too much oralization used throughout the upper range, with either no lower voice whatever, or a very limited lower range of heavy, raspy quality. The cure, be it man, woman, or child, is always the same: one tone production throughout the range, through the development of diaphragmatic breathing, clear tone, and adequate nasalization to create an efficient balance in muscular actions, so that the pitch mechanism can produce the complete range without breaks.

There is no apparent injury from falsetto singing, unless used so continuously that it becomes a permanent habit. It seems to have a very definite use in some voices as a means of developing the true mezzavoce in men, women, and children. Its lack of ability to crescendo without breaking, its very limited power, and its being confined to the upper voice and the upper half of the middle range (in most students), gives it little value, except for choral effects in male choirs, where the mezza-voce is still undeveloped, and as a possible bridging from altos to baritones in male choirs where the male section of basses is so strong that young voices might force their tones if allowed to continuously sing with the adults immediately after the voice change. It is the writer's personal opinion, however, that the mezza-voce tone should be developed in all voices as rapidly as possible and the falsetto abandoned, for any use of any kind. *It is merely an escape mechanism for untrained controls for producing high pitches.* The breathy tone is the principal cause of the register-break between the middle and upper range. Once the vocal lips have been trained to closure as in Figures E, F, and G of Plate III, the student, whatever the age or sex, will find that with correct nasalization the so-called registers have disappeared from the voice and that all gradations of tone from pianissimo to fortissimo are possible throughout the range.

It is a real joy to work with boys. The one rule necessary is that you put yourself in the boy's place and really like boys. If you do, you will find that they have the enthusiasm for really "delivering the goods." On the playground they literally yell and scream—their throats are tough, their vitality tense. The director who wishes to make good with a "gang" of boys must know his techniques so thoroughly that he can transfer that vitality into a beautifully resonant tone, without losing the boys' enthusiasm. The basic techniques of good posture, diaphragmatic breathing, abdominal lift in expiration, and clear tone from the light *m*-hum leading into the fully resonated *ä* vowel will change the natural blatant, yelling quality of any boy-group into beautiful tone, without loss of vitality in the tone color. Carried on into the practice of the English syllables as a vocalizing medium, freedom in articulation can be surely and steadily built.

The regular exercises of EMERGENT VOICE are unusually effective in boy-training. During the time the boy's voice is changing and his range is limited to the alto-tenor compass, the two following exercises should be substituted for Exercises 8 and 9 of Series II. They keep the boy from attempting to work in a longer range than is easy during the change of voice.

Exercise 8   Exercise 9

The age-old question of whether to allow the boy to sing during the time his voice is changing has a very simple answer. Certainly! Let him sing! But be sure you know enough about voices, so that you never allow him to use any muscle blocks during the changing period. Bad habits are very easily formed during this time, but there is no more reason for him to stop singing than there is for him to stop talking. You can't make him stop either. Watch for signs of tension such as scowling, thrusting out the jaw, straining the cords of the neck, tipping the head back, and the instant you see any of these signs have the boy move down one part—from soprano to alto, alto to alto-tenor, alto-tenor to tenor, tenor to baritone, baritone to low bass.

Nelson[1] completed a research in June, 1954, on 44 adolescents. This research was a comparison by X-rays, physical measurements (including height, weight, blood pressure, vital capacity, etc.) and tape recordings of their singing voices before and after an eight month training period. The vocal and tongue exercises of EMERGENT VOICE were used 3 times a week for training. In spite of enormous variations in individual growth, there was definite improvement in tone quality, normal vibrato, resonation, accuracy in articulation, and musical achievement.

The boy-choir director who discards old concepts of o͞o-vowel, hooty singing, and downward progressions with falsetto breathy tones, and begins with diaphragmatic breathing and the clear m-hum, using the same exercises as with adult voices, will ultimately reap a rich reward of beautiful, resonant, clear, vital singing by his boy-groups.

[1] Nelson, Russel Charles. *A Physiological Study of the Utilization of the Vital Capacity in Phonation, Resonation, and Articulation and its Effect on Tone Quality in the Adolescent.* Doctoral dissertation, University of Michigan, 1954.

Chapter XIV

INTERPRETATION AND LITERATURE

"In the symphony we are stirred by the beauties of
tone, in drama by words and actions, in song by a welding
of all three. Song appeals to the individual the strongest."

—DR. ALBERT A. STANLEY

WHEN a talented composer finds a bit of literature which strikes
his fancy, he studies it until all the thoughts, emotions, passions
and moods expressed by the words become so vivid to him, that
a melody springs into existence to increase that vividness. It may come
full-blown, a finished product, or he may need to study more carefully
the rhythm, accent, and emphasis of the words, the shades of meaning
within phrases, words, and syllables, to make his melody live as a
perfect unity with the message which the words wish to convey.

When the melody is completed, he starts the task of glorifying it
with an accompaniment which brings out in even greater beauty, each
shifting sentiment, so that the true meaning of the underlying emotion
may grip the imagination of the singer and his audience. The rhythmic
pulse, the melodic line, the changing tempos, the phrasing, the crescendos and decrescendos, the accents, the sustained legato flow or the
dynamic energy surges of sforzandos are all part of the tools which the
composer must use if he wishes to transfer to the singer, the inspiration
which came to him as a composer from the poem of his choice.

If a song is worthy of public performance, the student should use
the same care in memorizing and producing it, as the composer used
in its composition. It is easy to determine the worth of a composition.
Read the poem. Is the message worth repeating? Study the poem.
Does your interest in it increase? Examine the melodic line against
the word emphasis. Are the rhythmic pulse, the accents, and the melody
identical with the natural inflections used while reading the poem?
Study the accompaniment. Does it reinforce the thoughts, emotions,
passions, or moods expressed by the poem, the rhythms, the melody?
If the answer is *yes* to all of these questions you can be assured that
the composition is worthy of your best efforts in reproducing it. If
the student really wishes to become an artistic singer he must always
remember that *SINGING IS GLORIFIED SPEECH.*

Memorize your song in the same order in which it was composed.

The first step in interpretation, in vocal music, is the thorough
study and memorization of the words. This should always be done

with special emphasis on the meaning, the natural phrasing, the normal accent and rhythm, and the location of energy surges in their relationship to the overlapping and blending of the consonants between words. Before the student studies a melody, he should know the words of a vocal composition as thoroughly as the composer did when he was inspired to write a melody to those words.

The second step in interpretation of vocal music is the thorough memorization of the melody. This means perfect and exact memorization of the most minute details of time, notes, rests, phrase lengths, breathing, marks of expression, rates of tempo changes, and all dynamic markings, as well as the tune.

The third step is the welding together of the words and music until they become a unit for expressing every shade of sentiment and feeling intended by the author and the composer. In many modern compositions steps two and three must be done together, for it is musically impossible to memorize the melody without the accompaniment because of the many inharmonic changes.

The fourth step, and the most important from an artistic standpoint, is the student's own creative interpretation of the composition. Through his enthusiastic exuberance for the composition, he must recreate it as his own. No two individuals are alike. The student's interpretation of a composition for public performance will never be exactly as either the author or composer intended, if it is genuinely his own. It is mentally and physically impossible for even the same individual if he sings the same phrase twice, to sense an identical *emotion* felt in anger, sorrow, fear, joy, grief, hate, disgust, love, surprise, awe, yearning, reverence, and resentment; or an identical *passion* of fury, anguish, terror, hilarity, rage; or an identical *mood* of chagrin, gloom, anxiety, happiness, sullenness, moroseness; and the hundreds of other shades of feelings. We certainly can't expect him to sense these things in any way except as his experience in life, his imagination and his coach's enthusiastic interpretation have pictured them to him. If he is a true artist, his interpretation will shift with every performance. If his accompanist is a true artist, he will sense the changes as the number progresses, will assist the singer in making vivid many nuances which neither have felt before.

The basic law of interpretation is sensitive deviation *from the form of composition as written and memorized.*

Just as there are Arab and Percheron horses, Guernsey and Hereford cattle, Razor Back and Poland China pigs; so there are hyper- and hypothyroid, hyper- and hypoadrenal, and hyper- and hypopituitary families in the human race. The ability and wish to express our emotions before the public, depends largely on who our great-grandparents were. The author has seen many hyperthyroid, hyperadrenal voice teachers literally wear and tear themselves to shreds trying to get a hyperpituitary pupil to interpret a song in a way which was so absolutely foreign to the pupil's mental, nervous, and glandular make-up, that the pupil left the voice lesson in utter discouragement. The study of the student's personality is as essential as the study of his natural articulation, if the student is ever to develop *his personality and his interpretation* (not his teacher's) into full artistry.

Most of us have a mortal fear of actually "letting go" and throwing ourselves wholeheartedly into interpreting the sentiments which we should freely express in our singing. We have a fear that our friends will think that we are affected, trying to show off, or exaggerating the emotions of the song. The real fact is, that unless we forget ourselves in our enthusiasm for the song and its emotions, we are not truly artistic. The most beautiful voice in the world is a disappointment, without enthusiasm in interpretation. Some accepted artists actually have inferior vocal equipment, but do such marvelous work in interpretation, that the public becomes so interested in the emotions it feels, that it forgets the inferior voice.

Whenever a beautiful, flexible voice is combined with an unusual ability to interpret, then we recognize the artist as an outstanding performer of that generation. All musical history records only a few, sometimes only a single one in a whole generation, a Ferri, a Faranelli, a Rubini, a Caruso. We are constantly harped at in all vocal writing about the so-called "golden age of song." The development of simple techniques through scientific research is bringing us now to an age of singing so superior to any previously witnessed, that all past vocal achievements will be dwarfed into insignificance. The complete knowledge of the "why," "how," and "what" of every technique used will ultimately develop not one or two in a generation but thousands with the flexibility and ease of production attained by the few in the "golden age."

To become an *outstanding* artist, however, one needs a vivid personality, ability to interpret vocal literature with unbounded enthusiasm, exceptional musicianship, perseverance, unlimited ambition, enthusiasm, poise, assurance, and a deep emotional nature under perfect control, as well as an unusual voice. Some of the finest voices the human race has ever produced have remained unknown, because of some innate lack in the characteristics necessary to "put the voice across" to the public. Most of the necessary assets listed above can be developed, but not to the extent of truly great artistry, unless the natural equipment is of the best, for the road is too long and hard to travel if one is to reach the heights in one short lifetime. Not even the most unusual voice student should be given the false hope of international fame unless he is given with it, an accurate picture of the folk song, ballad, classical song, romantic song, art song, cantata, oratorio, musical comedy, light opera, grand opera, English, Italian, German, French, Russian, Spanish, Latin road he must travel. And please do not forget that the above list assumes that the student knows that he must have a basic knowledge of musical theory, piano-playing, rhythmic, melodic and harmonic sight-reading and all the knowledge of poetry, interpretative reading, and dramatics that he can attain. Only the most unusual voice, personality, musicianship and dramatic ability will make a truly great artist. The first two may be ancestral gifts but they will not be retained nor the last two developed without an *unbounded persevering enthusiasm* that drives the individual to the thorough, accurate, and painstaking completion of every task as he travels the road of building the vast repertoire necessary to continued popularity in public performance. *Beautiful singing in one's native tongue, for the pleasure and service which it gives, should be the goal of most teachers and students.* Ambition and the ability to reach the pinnacle of success lies with the few—the spark is within one's self—the equipment comes by inheritance, environment, and hard work. The voice student who wishes to rise to the heights, should do a good job in picking his great-grandparents, as well as his piano teacher, theory teacher, voice teacher, dramatic teacher, and repertoire coach.

If you are a voice student and the above paragraph discourages you, it has served its purpose, for you will never be a great artist anyway. If it inspires you to tackle the job, it has doubly served its purpose, for you have the stuff of which real artists are made.

The author has always had an intense feeling of antagonism toward the voice teacher who brazenly clamors about the student's chances at the "Met" in the next two or three years. Any student can go as far as his own enthusiasm, perseverance, natural talents and *the circumstances over which he has no control,* will permit him to go. Both the teacher and the student should remember constantly that throughout all the history of music the outstanding voices of any one type, at a given time, can always be named on one hand.

It is a sad commentary on the voice teaching profession, that throughout the whole history of music, more lovely natural voices have been ruined by poor teaching than have been built by good teaching. The voice student needs just one criterion by which he can judge his teacher. If a voice lesson makes you sing easier than you did before you took it, your teacher is all right. If your throat is tired at the end of a voice lesson you had better hunt for another teacher, for the only muscles that get tired when you are singing correctly are the muscles of the abdominal wall, *never the throat.* One of the best known voice teachers of musical history, who taught over seventy-five years and is still quoted by the profession as the "end all," "know all" of voice techniques, made practically his entire reputation on one voice which came to him already developed by someone else. On the other hand every voice teacher falls heir to some personalities and voices which are simply impossible, but if they are true teachers and really know their work, even these will show improvement as work continues, for anyone with normal hearing, a normal throat, lungs, diaphragm, abdominal wall, and moderate intelligence can learn to sing beautifully.

Excellent interpretation, however, demands an instrument which is developed so that it is never in the way of the soloist as he interprets his song, but is so resonant, free, and flexible that it responds to his slightest wish—instantly. Just as no tennis or golf champion wins without training, so no voice student acquires such flexibility without training. It must be developed. Unless one learns to sing with the easy, balanced, flexibility advocated in EMERGENT VOICE he will never acquire the ability to express his emotions throughout his range, with perfect freedom.

LITERATURE

The beginning voice student will wish to know, "What shall I sing?" The answer is, "Anything which you can sing freely and interpret well."

The field of voice literature is enormous. A good natural voice with long range can sing practically anything without injury to the throat, provided the student has the common sense to *buy the music in a key in which he can sing and interpret it the best.* One of the hardest tasks of voice teaching is for the teacher to see that the student with natural talent builds his musicianship as fast as he builds his voice. Too many times his lack of musicianship will keep him from progressing as fast as his voice itself is capable of going. Attempting to read new music beyond one's musicianship always results in conflicts between the three rhythms of breathing, heart beat, and nerve pulses, and throws cramps and blocks into the resonation and articulation musculatures. This may result in tensions which will enormously retard the true development of the voice.

The natural logical approach to song literature for the beginning voice student is through the folk songs of his native tongue. In the best folk songs we find both the form and substance of our finest music literature. Simple and genuine sentiments of love, pleasure, and suffering have been sung about and passed on to son and daughter for many generations until the accents, rhythms, phrasing, and melodic lines of the songs have been smoothed out by the added inspirations of thousands, as these songs have been shaped to their final forms.

As posture and respiration are the foundation of speaking and singing techniques, as heart beat, breath pulse, and nerve impulses are the basis of all rhythmic patterns, as the fundamental and overtone series are the background of all melodic and harmonic growth, so, in the knowledge of the folk songs of the world, lies the basic development of true musicianship with which the study of more advanced musical forms is made simple and sure. They have been tried and refined in the fires of home life, tribal life, national life, and international migrations. Within their simple beauties lie the germs of the finest symphonies. Our greatest composers have always used the unlimited resources of folk song literature for their inspiration.

The student who examines even the simple a-a-b-a form of "Drink to Me Only With Thine Eyes," "All Through the Night," and "The Last Rose of Summer" is already on the road to an understanding of form and beauty in sound. Even this small beginning will make a Beethoven Symphony unfold with greater clarity long before the student's theoretical knowledge could solve its intricacies. All forms of music have their source in the simple forms of folk songs; all melodic intervals and rhythmic patterns can be found in their basic beauties; all the thoughts, emotions, passions, and moods expressed in other musical forms are expressed in genuine refined beauty in the gems of folk song literature.

Every vocal student who wishes to travel the unending road toward perfect freedom of self-expression through singing, will find his artistry founded upon the rock of simplicity when it is built on a knowledge of the folk song literature of his native tongue.

It has been the purpose of EMERGENT VOICE to build techniques for practical *voice development,* for the study of the fundamentals of *musical theory* and for the study of *interpretation and literature,* all built on the basic causes of their emergence.

If the student will make the techniques of EMERGENT VOICE truly his own, he will be able to determine the motivation of every emotion, feeling, and sensation in the song he is studying; he will be able to determine how the rhythm and accent of the words actually built the rhythmic and melodic patterns of the song; he will be able to grasp the beauties of the simple forms of the finest folk song literature. With that equipment, he need have no fear of his ultimate success in his chosen field.

*   *   *   *

The following bibliography of American folk song literature is not intended to be exhaustive. It is compiled from many sources, but mostly from the materials graciously sent to the author by members of the "Music Education Exhibitors Association," from their publications of American Folk Songs. It is published at the close of EMERGENT VOICE in the hope that voice teachers, public school music teachers, and students will take advantage of the variety of songs available, to make such a worthy choice in poetic content, musical worth and suitability of range for class or individual, that they will develop and maintain an unending interest in the basic growth of a knowledge of fundamentals in singing.

There was in America a native music thousands of years old before white man first planted his feet upon the Western Hemisphere. It was developed as true folk songs have always been developed, from the life of the people. We put the songs of the American Indian first in our bibliography for they were first. To a great extent, the rest of the bibliography follows the colonization of America; the Sea Shanteys and Sailor Songs that brought us here; the Mountaineer Songs of the Atlantic seaboard; the Negro Songs of the South; the Creole Songs of the Mississippi settlements; the Spanish and Mexican Songs of California; the Lumber Jack and French Canadian Songs; the Cowboy Songs of the Great Plains. Then at the end, a small but thorough bibliography of the collections of the principal folk songs of the nations from which we sprang.

BIBLIOGRAPHY OF AMERICAN FOLK SONGS

COLLECTIONS OF AMERICAN INDIAN FOLK SONGS

BIMBONI, ALBERTO. Songs of the American Indians. G. Schirmer, New York, 1917.

BOTSFORD, FLORENCE H. The Botsford Collection of Folk Songs, Vol. I. G. Schirmer, New York.

BURTON, FREDERICK R. American Primitive Music. Moffet, Yard & Co., New York, 1909.

CRONYN, GEORGE W. The Path of the Rainbow, North American Indian Songs. Boni & Liveright, New York, 1918.

CURTIS, NATALIE. The Indian's Book. Harper and Bros., New York, 1907.

DENSMORE, FRANCES. Indian Action Songs. C. C. Birchard, 1921. American Indians and Their Music. Woman's Press, New York, 1936.

FLETCHER, ALICE C. Indian Games and Dances with Native Songs. C. C. Birchard, 1915.

GRUNN, HOMER. From Desert and Pueblo. Ditson (Presser), 1924.

KRONES, BEATRICE and MAX. Songs and Stories of our American Indians. Kjos.

LAMKIN, NINA B., and JAGENDORF, M. Around America with the Indian. Willis Music Co.

LIEURANCE, THURLOW B. Songs of the North American Indian. Presser Co., Philadelphia, 1920.

TROYER, CARLOS. Traditional Songs of the Zunis. Wa-Wan Press, Newton Center, Mass., 1904.

Many Solos by Bimboni, Cadman, Farwell, Lieurance, Loomis, Metcalf, etc.

SEA SHANTEYS AND SAILOR SONGS

BONE, D. W. Capstan Bars. Harcourt, Brace and Co., New York, 1932.

COLCORD, JOANNA C. Roll and Go. Bobbs-Merrill, Indianapolis, 1924.

CROSLEY, JOSEPH W. Book of Navy Songs. Doubleday-Page.

FROTHINGHAM, ROBERT. Songs of the Sea and Sailors' Shanties. Houghton Mifflin, Cambridge, 1924.

GOODELL, WALTER. Chanteys and Songs of the Sea. Hall and McCreary.

NEESER, ROBERT W. American Naval Songs and Ballads. Yale University Press, 1938.

RICKABY, FRANS. Ballads and Songs of the Shanty Boy. Harvard University Press.

SHARP, CECIL J. English Folk Chanteys. Simpkin, Marshall, Hamilton, Kent & Co., London, 1914.

SHAY, FRANK. Iron Men and Wooden Ships. Doubleday, Doran & Co., New York.

TERRY, SIR R. R. Sailor Shanties, Book I, Book II. J. Curwen & Sons, London, Bk. I, 1921; Bk. II, 1926.

WHALL, W. B. Sea Songs and Shanties. Brown & Son, Glasgow, 1920.

MOUNTAINEER SONGS

BARTHOLOMEW, MARSHALL. Mountain Songs of North Carolina. G. Schirmer, New York.

BROCKWAY, HOWARD. Lonesome Tunes (Kentucky). H. W. Gray.

HUGHES, ROBERT. Song from the Hills of Vermont. G. Schirmer, New York, 1919.

LOESSER, ARTHUR. Humor in American Songs. Howell, Soskin, New York, 1942.

LUNSFORD, BASCOM LAMAR, and LAMAR STRINGFIELD. 30 and 1 Folk Songs from the Southern Mountains. Carl Fischer, 1929.

MATTESON, MAURICE. Beach Mountain Folk Songs and Ballads (North Carolina). G. Schirmer, New York.

McGILL, JOSEPHINE. Folk Songs of the Kentucky Mountains. Boosey, New York, 1917.

NILES, JOHN JACOB. Seven Kentucky Mountain Songs. Songs of the Hill Folk. More Songs of the Hill Folk. Ten Appalachian Mountain Christmas Carols. G. Schirmer, New York.

POWELL, JOHN. Five Virginia Folk Songs. J. Fischer & Bros., New York, 1938.

RICHARDSON, ETHEL PARK, and SPAETH, SIGMUND. American Mountain Songs. Greenberg, New York, 1927.

SANDBURG, CARL. The American Songbag. Harcourt, Brace and Co., New York, 1927.

SHARP, CECIL J. Appalachian Mountain Songs, 1st and 2nd Series. 1st Series: American-English Folk Songs, G. Schirmer, 1918. 2nd Series: Folk Songs of English Origin, Novello, London, 1921. English Folk Songs from the Southern Appalachians, G. P. Putnam's Sons, New York.

STURGIS, EDITH, and HUGHES, ROBERT. Songs from the Hills of Vermont. G. Schirmer, New York, 1919.

THOMAS, JEAN. Devil's Ditties. Wilbur Hatfield, Chicago, Ill.

WETMORE, SUSANNAH, and BARTHOLOMEW, MARSHALL. Mountain Songs of North Carolina. G. Schirmer, New York, 1926.

WHEELER, MARY. Kentucky Mountain Folk Songs. Willis Music Co., Cincinnati, Ohio.

WYMAN, LORAINE, and BROCKWAY, HOWARD. Lonesome Tunes, H. W. Gray, New York, 1916. Twenty Kentucky Mountain Songs, Oliver Ditson, 1920.

NEGRO FOLK SONGS

BOTSFORD, FLORENCE H. Botsford Collection of Folk Songs, Vol. I. G. Schirmer, New York, 1931.

BURLEIGH, HARRY T. Negro Folk Songs, G. Ricordi, New York, 1921. Negro Spirituals, Vols. I and II, G. Ricordi, New York, 1917-1922.

BURLIN, NATALIE CURTIS. Negro Folk Songs (for Male Quartet). G. Schirmer, New York, 1918-1919.

DANN, HOLLIS. Twenty-one Spirituals. C. C. Birchard, Boston.

DANN, HOLLIS, with LOOMIS, HARVEY W. Fifty-eight Spirituals. C. C. Birchard, Boston.

DETT, NATHANIEL. Negro Spirituals, Vols. I, II, and III. John Church Co., Cincinnati, Ohio, 1919.

DITON, CARL. Thirty-six South Carolina Spirituals. G. Schirmer, New York, 1928.

DITSON, OLIVER. Jubilee and Plantation Songs. Oliver Ditson, 1887.

FISHER, WM. ARMS. Seventy Negro Spirituals. Oliver Ditson, Boston, 1926.

FISHER, WM. ARMS; GAUL, HARVEY; JOHNSON, J. ROSAMOND; and MANNEY, CHARLES FONTEYN. Ten Negro Spirituals. Oliver Ditson, 1925.

GAUL, HARVEY B. Nine Negro Spirituals. H. W. Gray, New York, 1918.

GOODELL, WALTER. Forty-two Popular Spirituals. Hall & McCreary Co., Chicago.

GUION, DAVID. Darkey Spirituals. M. Witmark & Sons, New York, 1918.

HALLOWELL, EMILY. Calhoun Plantation Songs (Male Quartet). C. W. Thompson Co., Boston, 1907.

JACKSON, MARYLOU. Negro Spirituals and Hymns (Women's Trio). J. Fischer & Bros., New York.

JOHNSON, HALL. The Green Pastures, Carl Fischer, New York. The Green Pasture Spirituals, Farrar & Rinehart, New York, 1930.

JOHNSON, J. ROSAMOND. Rolling Along in Song, E. C. Schirmer, Boston. Utica Jubilee Singers Spirituals (Male), Oliver Ditson, Boston, 1930.

JOHNSON, JAMES WELDON and J. ROSAMOND. The Book of American Negro Spirituals, 1925. The Second Book of American Negro Spirituals, 1940. Viking Press, New York. The Book of American Negro Spirituals, 1944.

KREHBIEL, HENRY E. Afro-American Folk Songs. G. Schirmer, New York, 1914.

MARSH, J. B. T. The Story of the Jubilee Singers. Houghton, Osgood & Co., Boston, 1880.

NILES, JOHN J. Seven Negro Exultations, G. Schirmer, New York. Impressions of a Negro Camp Meeting, Carl Fischer, New York.

SANDBURG, CARL. The American Songbag. Harcourt, Brace & Co., New York.

SEWARD, T. F. Jubilee Songs. Biglow, Main & Co., New York, 1872.

TAYLOR, JEAN. Six Spirituals. H. W. Gray Co., New York.

WHITE, CLARENCE C. Negro Folk Melodies, 1927. Forty Negro Spirituals, Theo. Presser Co., Philadelphia.

WORK, FREDERICK H. Folk Songs of the American Negro, 1907. New Jubilee Songs, 1902. Fisk University Press, Nashville, Tenn.

WORK, JOHN WESLEY. Folk Songs of the American Negro. Fisk University Press, Nashville, Tenn., 1915.

CREOLE FOLK SONGS

CABLE, GEO. W. Creole Slave Songs. Century, New York, 1886.

FEDERAL THEATRE PROJECT. Folk Tunes from Mississippi (pamphlet). Fed. Theatre Proj., Washington, D.C., 1937.

HARE, MAUD CUNEY. Six Creole Folk Songs. Carl Fischer, New York, 1921.

LOMAX, JOHN A., and LOMAX, ALAN. American Ballads and Folk Songs. Macmillan Co., New York, 1935.

MONROE, MINA, and SCHINDLER, KURT. Bayou Ballads. G. Schirmer, New York, 1921.

PETERSON, CLARA GOTTSCHALK. Creole Songs. L. Gruenwald Co., New Orleans, 1902.

SPANISH AND MEXICAN FOLK SONGS OF THE SOUTHWEST

FARWELL, ARTHUR. Folk Songs of the West and South. Wa-Wan Press, Newton Center, Mass., 1905.

HAGUE, ELEANOR. Spanish-American Folk Songs. J. J. Augustin, New York, 1938.

HAGUE, ELEANOR, and ROSS, G. Early Spanish-Californian Folk Songs. J. Fischer and Bro., New York.

LOMAX, JOHN A., and LOMAX, ALAN. American Ballads and Folk Songs. Macmillan, New York, 1934.

LUMMIS, CHAS. F., and FARWELL, ARTHUR. Spanish Songs of Old California. G. Schirmer, New York.

SANDBURG, CARL. The American Songbag. Harcourt, Brace & Co., New York, 1927.

VAN STONE, M. R. Spanish Folk Songs of New Mexico. R. F. Seymour, Chicago, 1926.

LUMBERJACK AND CANADIAN FOLK SONGS

BARBEAU, C. M., and SAPIR, E. Folk Songs of French Canada. Yale University Press, New Haven, Conn., 1925.

BARBEAU, M., ENGLAND, P., and WILLAN, HEALY. Chanson Canadienne, Vols. I and II. Boston Music Co., 1929.

BOTSFORD, FLORENCE H. Botsford Collection of Folk Songs. G. Schirmer, New York, 1930.

GIBBON, J. MURRAY. Canadian Folk Songs. E. P. Dutton, 1927.

GRANT-SCHAEFFER, G. A. French-Canadian Songs. A. P. Schmidt Co., New York.

KARPELES, MAUD. Folk Songs from Newfoundland, Vols. I and II. Oxford University Press.

MACKENZIE, W. ROY. Ballads and Sea Songs from Nova Scotia. Harvard University Press, 1928.

SANDBURG, CARL. The American Songbag. Harcourt, Brace & Co., New York, 1927.

O'HARA, GEOFFREY. Seven Songs of Old Quebec. White-Smith, Boston.

SOMERVELL, ARTHUR. Twelve French-Canadian Folk Songs. Boosey and Hawkes.

TIERSOT, J. Forty-four French and Canadian Folk Songs. G. Schirmer, New York.

COWBOY SONGS AND THE WESTERN FRONTIER

CLARK. The Cowboy Sings. Paull-Pioneer, 1932.

FARWELL, ARTHUR. Folk Songs of the West and South. From Mesa and Plain. Wa-Wan Press, Newton Center, Mass., 1905.

FINGER, C. J. Frontier Ballads. Doubleday, Page & Co., New York, 1927.

HULBERT, A. B. Forty-Niners. Little, Brown and Co., Boston, 1932.

LARKIN, MARGARET, and BLACK, H. Singing Cowboy. Alfred Knopf, New York, 1931.

LOMAX, JOHN A., and LOMAX, ALAN. Cowboy Songs and Other Frontier Ballads: Macmillan Co., New York, 1937.

LOMAX, JOHN A. Songs of the Cattle Trail and Cow Camp. Macmillan Co., New York, 1919.

SANDBURG, CARL. The American Songbag. Harcourt, Brace and Co., New York, 1927.

SHERWIN, STERLING, and KATZMAN, LOUIS. Songs of the Goldminers. Carl Fischer, New York, 1932.

SIRES, INA. Songs of the Open Range. C. C. Birchard, Boston, 1928.

THORPE, N. H. Songs of the Cowboys. Houghton Mifflin Co., Boston, 1921.

WHITE, JOHN, and SHACKLEY, GEO. The Lonesome Cowboy. Geo. T. Worth, New York, 1930.

MISCELLANEOUS FOLK SONGS

BANTOCK, GRANVILLE. Sixty Patriotic Songs of All Nations. One Hundred Folk Songs of All Nations. Oliver Ditson.

BONI. Fireside Series. Folk Songs. American Songs. Simon & Schuster, 1947.

BOTSFORD, FLORENCE HUDSON. Botsford Collection of Folk Songs, Vols. I, II and III, 1931-33. The Universal Folk Songster, 1937. G. Schirmer, New York.

BURK, CASSEY, 1892. MIERHOFFER, VIRGINIA, and PHILLIPS, C. A. America's Musical Heritage. Laidlaw, 1942.

CARMER, CARL. America Sings, Alfred A. Knopf, New York, 1942. Songs of the Rivers of America, Farrar & Rinehart, New York, 1942.

CASTAGNETTA, GRACE, and VAN LOON, H. W. Folk Songs of Many Lands. Simon & Schuster, 1938.

DAVIS, KATHERINE WALLACE. Cradle Songs of Many Nations. Clayton F. Summy Co., Chicago, 1936.

ELSON, LOUIS C. Folk Songs of Many Nations. John Church Co. (Presser), Philadelphia, 1905.

EWEN, DAVID. Songs of America. Zeff-Davis, 1947.

FOSTER, STEPHEN C. Twenty Songs, Oliver Ditson Co., 1906, 1936. Album of Songs, G. Schirmer, New York.

FREEMAN, LEAVITT. Songs to Sing. Ginn, 1943.

GILBERT, H. F. B. One Hundred Folk Songs from Many Countries. C. C. Birchard, Boston, 1910.

HELD, CONRAD. Fifteen Shaker Songs. G. Schirmer, 1944.

IVES, BURL. Burl Ives Tales of America. Burl Ives Song Book. World Pub.

JOHNSON, MARGARET and TRAVIS. Early American Songs. Associated Music Pub., 1943.

KOLB, SYLVIA and JOHN. Treasury of Folk Songs. Bantam No. 123.

LANDECK, BEATRICE. Songs to Grow On, 1950. More Songs to Grow On. Songs My True Love Sings, 1946. E. B. Marks.

LEONARD, BAUM, MOORE. American Music Horizons. Silver Burdett.

LOMAX, ALLAN. Our Singing Country. Vol. II. Macmillan, 1941.

LUND, ENGEL. Book of Folk Songs. Oxford University Press (Carl Fischer), 1936.

LUTHER, FRANK. Americans and Their Songs. Harper & Bros., New York.

MACCARTENEY. A Child's Book of American Songs. Willis, 1931.

MATTESON. American Folk Songs for Young Singers. G. Schirmer.

MURILLO, ERNESTO. National Anthems of North, Central, and South America. Clayton F. Summy, Chicago, 1935.

OFFICER, HARVEY. Folk Songs of the Four Seasons. G. Schirmer, New York, 1929.

PARISH, LYDIA. Slave Songs of the Georgia Sea Islands. Creative Age Press, Inc., New York, 1942.

RADCLIFFE-WHITEHEAD, JANE BYRD. Folk Songs and Other Songs for Unison Singing. Oliver Ditson, 1927.

SANDBURG, CARL. The American Songbag. Harcourt, Brace and Co., New York, 1927.

G. SCHIRMER. Schirmer's American Folk Song Series. 20 sets. G. Schirmer, New York.

SEEGER, RUTH. American Folk Songs for Children, 1948. Animal Folk Songs for Children. American Folk Songs for Christmas, 1950. Doubleday & Co.

SEMBRICH, MARCELLA. My Favorite Folk Songs (Low Voice). Oliver Ditson, 1918.

SHARP, CECIL JAMES. American-English Folk Songs, First Series, G. Schirmer, 1918. Folk Songs—Various Countries, Novello & Co., London (H. W. Gray). One Hundred Folk Songs, Oliver Ditson.

SMITH, REED, and RUFTY, HILTON. American Anthology of Old World Ballads. J. Fischer & Bro., New York, 1937.

WAITE, H. R. College Songs. Oliver Ditson, 1887.

WILSON, H. R. Songs of the Hills and Plains. Hall & McCreary, 1943.

WILSON, HUNTINGTON. Sing and Dance. Hall & McCreary, 1945.

(Reprinted from JOURNAL OF SPEECH DISORDERS, Vol. 6, No. 4, December, 1941)

THE VIBRATO: A SPECIFIC INTEGRATIONAL EMERGENCE UPON FUSURE OF SOMATIC RHYTHMS [1]

KENNETH N. WESTERMAN

THERE have been, since the turn of the century, many investigations in vibrato,[2] that rhythmic pulsation heard in the human voice, particularly when produced by trained singers. These investigations were confined almost entirely to its perception and the physical aspects of the rate, amplitude, and complexity of its wave forms.

Believing that the human voice, to the producer, has its causation, transmission, and perception in physiological functions, the present investigation was made from the standpoint of the physiological actions which produce vibrato. The contribution of the present investigation, if any, lies in the search for:

1. The somatic rhythms which are fused in the emergent vibrato.

2. The muscular actions in the voice-producing mechanism which assist in that fusure.

This study of the specific integrational emergence of vibrato in the human voice was made through an objective examination of the effects upon the voice of physiological actions in the framework of tonus, tetany, contracture, and simple contraction.

It was already known through previous investigations that vibrato consisted of more or less regular pulsations of three separate cycles: rate, amplitude, and complexity. In perception, these three cycles are recognizable as pulsing variations in pitch, intensity, and timbre.

It was self-evident that three things would be of vast importance to a causative investigation:

1. A thorough knowledge of the tonic innervation of gross skeletal muscles, in order to know the source of the rates found.

2. A thorough knowledge of the framework of tonus, tetany, contracture, and simple contraction in order to determine certain basic techniques for experimentation.

3. Adequate machinery for permanently recording the vibrations in the voices of subjects, so that the results of physiological actions could be studied at leisure.

---

[1] An epitome of a dissertation submitted in partial fulfillment of the requirements for the degree of Doctor of Science in the University of Michigan, June 27, 1938. Dr. John H. Muyskens, Chairman, Committee.

[2] See bibliography at end of article.

An exhaustive investigation, covering all available sources of research in the action currents innervating the muscles of the human body, brought the following facts to light.[3]

1. The source of tonus is from the muscle itself. This is constantly proven by its complete loss, on section of either its receptor (afferent) nerve or its effector (motor, efferent) nerve.

2. Tonus is the controlling mechanism for the fixation of gross skeletal musculatures. This is shown by the fact that its action current rates of 5, 7, and 10 per second are found as a background in muscles showing active contraction rates of 20, 40, 50, and 100 per second.

3. Physiological tremor and tonus are identical and form the normal background of all postural muscular activity.

4. Clinical tremor and hypertonicity are exaggerations of this mechanism; caused by physiological conditions destroying its normal emergence.

5. Action currents are of vibrato rates in physiological tremor, tonic contractions, and in tetany of gross skeletal muscles in a condition of balanced flexibility.

6. Reflex tonicity, expressing itself in the somatic rhythms shown in the action currents of muscles in postural activity, is in reality, a fusure of receptor nerve impulses through the co-ordinating functioning of cerebellar, vestibular, lenticular, cortical, and rubro-spinal nerve paths, for the efficient maintenance of active posture.

The contributions of physiology to our problem are of inestimable worth, for they bring to us, not only the facts of somatic rhythms at vibrato rates, but the framework of the muscular actions which carry those rhythms in both normal and clinical forms. *They showed that when the tetanic contraction of gross skeletal muscles of posture, as fixating muscles of primitive levers, according to the scale of tonus, tetany, contracture, and simple contraction, functioning phasically with the smaller adjunct contracture groups of respiration, permit the simple contractions of the selective action of the minimal motors of phonation and articulation, a normal vibrato should emerge.*

The techniques used and the data examined resulted from the above working hypothesis.

For recording the voices of subjects, a velocity type radio microphone, standard commercial amplifiers, and recording cutter were used. The motor driving the recording turntable was a synchronous motor, which maintained a constant turntable speed at all times. The same was used as a play-back when pictures were made. The amplifiers were capable of faithful reproduction over a frequency range of 40 to 10,000 cycles per second and the recorder from 40 to 6,000 cycles per second.

---

[3] See bibliography for main sources of information.

This range was sufficient for any tone complexity in overtones of any value in examination.

In the matter of machinery for examining the record of voices, of the subjects used in the investigations, an enormous amount of experimentation was carried on.

Because of the chance of mechanical losses in transmission, the phoneloscope and phonodyke types were finally discarded as not being sensitive enough for perfect recordings. Experimentations with the cathode-ray oscillograph finally resulted in the construction, by Jerome Weisner of the Electrical Engineering School, of a special oscillograph, designed for this investigation, with a controlled anode potential from 1200 to about 3000 volts. This made possible a brilliancy in light which made the photographing of the records both distinct and accurate.

A high-speed camera from the University Heart Station was used for making the pictures. Since the original research, a new high-speed camera has been built for the investigator by the University Physics Instrument Shop, with special gear shift and synchronous motor, so that either the slow forms of action currents or the minute details of fundamental and overtones may be studied in the wave form. The three accompanying pictures show a typical vibrato wave form of a trained soloist and the same wave form at the antinode and node of a single form at the higher speed, and larger amplification. The first

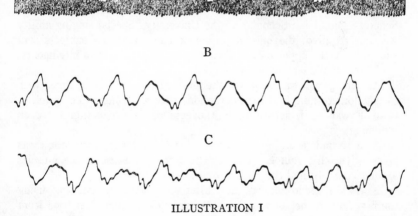

A

B

C

ILLUSTRATION I

VIBRATO

A. E vowel vibrato at slow speed.
B. Same vibrato at high speed and great amplitude showing the form at an antinode.
C. Same vibrato at high speed showing form at the node.

shows the vibrato; the second and third shows fundamental and over-tones, at the antinode and node positions of a single vibrato wave form. The vowel is an $\bar{e}$.

To disassociate vibrato emergence from psychological aspects and the already disproven "emotional tension" working hypothesis, of the early Iowa researches, the investigator made some preliminary examinations under physiological conditions which could not possibly be construed as emotional. The vibratos of trained singers were examined from simple *m-* *n-* and *ng*-hums before and after violent exercise. (Twenty-two subjects were used. Adult students and teachers of voice attending the University Summer School, students at the University School of Music, and voice students of the investigator.) The results were overwhelming. Vibrato regularity and control were exactly in proportion to each student's ability as an athlete to control the balanced, flexible use of his muscles. Track men, basketball players, swimmers, tennis players, football players, all showed practically the same tonic controls before and after exercise. Overweight, sedentary, flabby individuals, with good vibratos before exercise, completely lost control after exercise, their vibratos taking on active contraction rates, instead of those of tonic innervation.

Considerable thought was given to the techniques to be used in the examination of the physiological emergent framework of tonus, tetany, contracture, and simple contraction as expressed in posture, respiration, phonation, and articulation.

It was decided that a good cross section of voices could be found by examining groups of subjects from the 5th Grade, Junior High School, Senior High School, and the University. Special singing ability was not required, the only requirement being that the subjects sent should be in the upper half of their respective groups as to intelligence.

Three simple techniques were used:

1. The group was sent by the microphone, one at a time, with instructions to hum into the microphone with an *m*-hum. The pitch of C or F was used, according to the ease of its production for each individual.

2. A second recording was made after the following instruction was given—"Just lift your chest enough to free up the use of the muscles around your ribs and the wall of your stomach."

3. A third recording was made after some practice, humming, using the first half of the colloquial yes "mhm" to acquire a clear tone from normal spoken controls.

The *m*-hum was used for all subjects and all techniques because of its lack of any muscular tension in articulation or vowel form, to interfere with the simple wave form of the pitch used by each individual.

Three reports were taken into consideration with each subject. The report which the student gave of his own experience as a vocalist; the perception notes which the investigator made during the recording of each subject; and the objective findings of the developed film through careful examination with calipers and transparent millimeter rule. These three reports were made as separate projects and no co-ordination done until they were all completed. For further verification, the records were played and compared with the developed film. This was done by two trained musicians with no reference to the other three reports. Thus the reports as finally given, are the objective reports of scientific measurement, doubly verified through the two-way subjective reports of perception. The perception reports were practically identical with the scientific measurements. Where there was the slightest variation, the objective measurement was used.

The following report for a group of 54 subjects examined, shows the effects of the simple techniques of posture and clear tone upon the emerging vibrato.

Before giving the techniques of posture and clear tone:

> 6 showed regular vibrato
> 33 irregular vibrato
> 15 with no vibrato or questioned
>
> ——
>
> 54 subjects

After following the instructions in posture and clear tone:

> 46 showed regular vibrato
> 6 irregular vibrato
> 2 questioned vibrato
>
> ——
>
> 54 subjects

We note that 24 subjects developed *amplitude* vibrato by the use of the *posture* technique only, and that 20 subjects developed *pitch* vibrato by the use of the *clear tone* technique; although 7 developed *pitch* vibrato by the use of the *posture* technique. Subjects Nos. 40, 43, 45, and 48 (all with pitch vibrato before any instructions were given), lost their pitch vibrato with the emergence of amplitude vibrato on the *posture* technique, but regained the pitch vibrato on the *clear tone* technique.

That the above are very definite indices that *amplitude vibrato* emerges from respiratory controls and the *pitch ·vibrato* from the mechanism of laryngeal pitch, when used in the production of clear tones, is not to be overlooked.

A report of the effect of posture and clear tone techniques upon the group of 16 Junior High students is even more significant.

Before instructions were given:
4 were with no vibrato.
12 with irregular vibrato.
By following the instructions in posture and clear tone production:
15 of the 16 developed regular vibrato of some type.
10 developed *amplitude* vibrato by use of the *posture* technique.
7 developed *pitch* vibrato *by* use of the *posture* technique.
12 developed *pitch* vibrato by use of the *clear tone* technique.

The emergence of the amplitude vibrato from the posture technique, which gave freedom to the balanced, flexible use of the musculatures of the respiratory mechanism, and the emergence of pitch vibrato from the clear tone technique, when "the vocal lips are approximated under mutual pressure laterally by the tonus of, and by the bulk of the thyro-arytenoid muscle aided by the structures lateral to it" [4] are both indices that the laws of structure and function are at work in vibrato emergence, and that the surges of energy through the pulses of tonus, tremor, and tetany of regulated respiration are responsible for amplitude vibrato, while the balanced flexibility of the intrinsic musculatures of phonation, with their regulating action currents are reflected in the pitch vibrato.

It is reasonable to expect that future investigations may show that complexity vibrato emerges from the effect upon the tone wave of musculatures controlling resonation and articulation. Empirical findings of the writer during his 25 years' experience as a voice teacher have shown many cases of pulsations of uvula, soft palate, pharyngeal muscles, cheeks, tongue, and lips. Any of these would reflect in the complexity of the tone wave through pulsing changes in the structure of the human resonator.

From the indices of the present investigation and the laws of adequacy in structure and function, the following findings are tentatively given with a full realization that future research on many subjects may verify the above thesis.

1. When the fixation muscles of back, neck, and shoulder girdle, with the adjunct musculatures of the thoracic cage, allow the selective action of the muscles of the diaphragm and abdomen to function with a balanced flexibility in respiration, a normal, artistic *amplitude* vibrato will emerge.

2. When the fixation muscles of the human larynx, with the adjunct muscles of its cartilaginous framework, allow the minimal motors of the intrinsic muscles of phonation to function with a balanced flexibility against the power mechanism of respiration, a normal, artistic *pitch* vibrato will emerge.

3. When the fixation muscles of the head and jaw, with the adjunct musculatures of pharynx, nasopharynx, and fauces allow the minimal

4 Bibliography, Strong.

motors of lips, tongue, and soft palate to function with a balanced flexibility in full resonation of the tone produced, a normal, artistic *complexity* vibrato will emerge.

4. When the gross skeletal muscles of posture and breath control, beautifully balanced in condition of tonus and tetany, are *phasically* functioning against the minimal motors of the delicately varying small muscles of larynx, pharynx, jaw, palate, tongue, and lips, an artistic vibrato emerges.

The above findings constitute the fundamental framework of the teaching of voice through an exact knowledge of the muscle movements involved in its emergence. These surges of energy from the musculatures of posture, respiration, valving, swallowing, sucking, and chewing, as they apply to breath control, phonation, resonation, and articulation in the emergence of the human voice, constitute the motor psychology on which the patterning and conditioning of the student as a producer absolutely depends.

BIBLIOGRAPHY

ADRIAN, E. D. Med. Sci. Abst. and Rev. 1920, Vol. II. 454.

ARIÖNS-KAPPERS, C. U., with G. CARL HUBER and ELIZABETH CAROLINE CROSBY. The Comparative Anatomy of the Nervous System of Vertebrates, Including Man. 1936, Vol. I and II.

BARTHOLOMEW, WILMER T. Acoustics of Music. Prentice Hall, 1946.

BARTON, E. H. A Text-Book on Sound. 1908.

BINET. Recherche sur le tremblement, Thésé de Paris. 1918.

BLOOMER, HENRY HARLAN. A Method of Determination of the Diaphragmatic Factor in Respiration. Thesis, University of Michigan. 1935.

BRODY, VIOLA A. An Experimental Study of the Emergence of the Process Involved in the Production of Song. Doctoral Dissertation, Univ. of Mich., 1947.

BRONK, D. W., with L. K. FERGUSON. The nervous control of intercostal respiration. University of Pennsylvania, September 4, 1934. Amer. Journ. Phys., Vol. 110, 700-707.

BUSQUET, H. Le Tremblement Physiologique, Thésé de Paris. 1904.

BUYTENDYK. Ztschr. F. Biol. 1913, lix. 36.

COMAN, FRANCIS DANA. Johns Hopkins University, Observations on the Relation of the Sympathetic Nervous System to Skeletal Muscle Tone. J. Hopkins Bul., Vol. 38. 1926.

DE KLEIJN, with R. MAGNUS. Pflügers Archiv. 1912.

EASELY, ELEANOR. A Comparison of the Vibrato in Concert and Opera Voices. Thesis, University of Iowa. 1929.

GEMELLI, AGOSTINE, with GUISEPPINA PASTORI. "L'Analisi Elettroacustica Del Linguaggio," Milano. 1934.

GOMEZ, D. M., with FERNAND LÉVY. "Essai Sur Le Tonus Du Muscle Squelettique," Revue Generale; Gazette Des Hopitaux, Vol. 109, No. 42, May 23, 1936.

HELMHOLTZ, HERMANN. Sensations of Tone, Translation, Alexander J. Ellis.

INGVAR, S. 1919. Zur Phyl. und Ontogonese Des Kleinhirns, Folia neur.-biol. Bd. II, S205.

JEANS, SIR JAMES HOPEWOOD. Science and Music. 1937.

KWALWASSER, JACOB. The Vibrato, Psychol. Monog. 36, 1926. No. I, 84-108.

LÉVY, FERNAND. Le Tremblement, Revue Generale; Gazette Des Hopitaux, Vol. 110, No. 1, January, 1937.

METFESSEL, MILTON. The Vibrato in Artistic Voices, University of Iowa Studies in Psychology of Music, Vol. I, The Vibrato. 1932.

MILLER, DAYTON C. Science of Musical Sounds. 1916.

MILLER, D. C. Sound Waves, Their Shape and Speed. 1937.

MUYSKENS, JOHN HENRY. The Hypha. Thesis, University of Michigan. 1925.

MUYSKENS, J. H. The Emergent Voice, The Year Book, Mus. Ed. Jour. 1938.

NELSON, RUSSEL CHARLES. A Physiological Study of the Utilization of the Vital Capacity in Phonation, Resonation, and Articulation, and Its Effect on Tone Quality in the Adolescent. Doctoral Dissertation, Univ. of Mich., 1954.

PALMER, MARTIN F. The Cardiac Cycle as a Physiological Determinant of Energy Distribution in Speech, Sp. Mon. 4:110-126. 1937.

RIDER, JOHN F. The Cathode Ray at Work. 1935.

RIJLANT, PIERRE. University of Brussels, Journ. Physiol. 80, Proc. 20, 1933. Ann. Physiol. Psychol. Biol. 9, 843.

RILEY, H. A., with F. TILNEY. The Form and Functions of the Central Nervous System. 1921.

SCHOEN, MAX. The Pitch Factor in Artistic Singing, Psychol. Monog. 31, 1922, No. I, 230-259.

SEASHORE, CARL E. University of Iowa Studies in Psychology of Music, Vol. III, Psychol. of the Vibrato in Voice and Instrument, February, 1936.

SEASHORE, H. G., with J. TIFFIN. Summary of the Established Facts in Experimental Studies of Vibrato up to 1932. University of Iowa Stud. Psych. Music, I. 1932.

SHERRINGTON, C. S. Postural Activity of Muscle and Nerve, 1915. Brain, Vol. 38, pp. 191, 202, 233, etc.

SHOHARA, HIDE. Genesis of the Articulatory Movements of Speech with Special Reference to the Processes of Sucking, Chewing, and Swallowing. Thesis, University of Michigan. 1932.

SMITH, OLIVE C. Harvard Medical School, Amer. Journ. Phys. Vol. 108, p. 629. 1934.

STRONG, LEON HENRI. The Mechanism of Laryngeal Pitch, The Anatomical Record, Vol. 63, No. I, August, 1935.

TIFFIN, J. The role of pitch and intensity in the vocal vibrato of students and artists. University of Iowa Stud. Psychol. Music, Vol. I. 1932.

WAGNER, ARNOLD. Remedial and Artistic Development of the Vibrato, University of Iowa Stud. in Psychol. Music, Vol. I, The Vibrato. 1932.

WEED, L. Journ. of Physiol. 1914, Vol. 48, p. 205.

WESTERMAN, K. N. Modern Phonetization Applied to Singing. 1936.

WESTERMAN, K. N. The Physiology of Vibrato, Music Educators Journal, March, 1938, p. 48-49.

WESTLAKE, HAROLD. The Mechanics of Phonation, An X-Ray Study of the Larynx. Thesis, University of Michigan, April, 1938.

WILSON, S. A. K. Progressive Lenticular Degeneration, Brain, Vol. 34. 1912.

WRIGHT, MUYSKENS, STRONG, WESTERMAN, KINGERY, WILLIAMS. A Study of the Tongue in Relation to Denture Stability. J. A. D. A., Sept., 1949.

MINNESOTA BIBLE COLLEGE
LIBRARY